ABOUT THE AUTHOR

Richard M. Salsman is a vice president and economist at H. C. Wainwright & Co. Economics, Inc., an economic forecasting firm based in Boston. Prior to joining Wainwright he was a banker in New York City. Mr. Salsman is the author of "Breaking the Banks: Central Banking Problems and Free Banking Solutions" (*Economic Education Bulletin*, AIER, June 1990), as well as numerous articles on money, banking, and economics.

EDITOR'S PREFACE

We are pleased to publish Mr. Salsman's "Gold and Liberty." This replaces earlier AIER publications on the history and significance of gold (previously published under the title "Why Gold?"). The current work benefits from, and includes some of the lessons of, the experience of the past quarter century of worldwide fiat currencies. Its major focus, however, is the importance of the evolution of gold-based money to human advancement and, even more significantly, to human freedom.

Readers who have followed our publications closely may recognize that Mr. Salsman's methodology differs in some respects from AIER's procedures of inquiry. Nevertheless, we believe this booklet shows what the arbitrary manipulation of the medium of exchange by unelected and unaccountable central bankers really means for ordinary citizens and points the way to useful reform.

Kerry A. Lynch
Director of Research and Education

Contents

INTRODUCTION 1
A Strange New World — Without Gold Money 1
Gold is a *Precious* Metal 2
The Modern Appeal of Gold 2
Gold and Economic Freedom 3

I. THE ORIGINS OF GOLD AS MONEY 5
The Convergence on Gold 5
Gold as the Money of Choice 8
Currency Units as Fixed Weights of Gold 9
Gold as an Objective Value 10
The Alleged "Mystical Qualities" of Gold 11
Gold and Exploration 12

II. FREE BANKING AND GOLD 15
Private Mints, Money Changers, and Goldsmiths 15
The Evolution of Free Banking 17
Free Banking and Economic Development 20
Free Banking in History 21
Myths About Free Banking 23

III. THE GOLD STANDARD IN THEORY 25
A Standard of Value 25
Like No Other Commodity 26
The Golden Constant 26
The Economics of Gold Mining 32
Prices, Cycles, and Growth Under the Gold Standard 33
Public Finance Under the Gold Standard 38

IV. THE CLASSICAL GOLD STANDARD 41
A Gold Coin Standard 41
How the Classical Gold Standard Worked 42
Free Banking versus Central Banking 45
A Century of Sound Money 45
Economic Effects of the Classical Gold Standard 47
International Economic Integration 48

V. POLITICAL AND LEGAL ISSUES 51
The Meaning of Gold 51
Gold and Property Rights 52
Constitutional Aspects of Gold 54
Gold and Liberty 58
The Imposition of Legal Tender Laws 60
The Criminalization of Gold Ownership 62

  VI. **SUBVERSION OF THE GOLD STANDARD** 65
      The Monetary Dissolution of World War I 65
      The Gold Exchange Standard 66
      Gold and the Great Depression 67
      The "Gold Shortage" Myth 69
      Government Defaults on the Gold Standard 71
      The Bretton Woods System and Its Aftermath 73
      Recent Failed Attempts at Unified Money 78

  VII. **CENTRAL BANKING AND GOLD** 81
      Central Banking: A Form of Central Planning 81
      The Incompatibility of Central Banking
         and the Gold Standard 88
      The Destructiveness of Inflating and Deflating 93
      Modern Defenders of Central Banking 95

VIII. **GOLD AS A BAROMETER AND INVESTMENT** 101
      The Gold Price: A Barometer of Paper Money Values 101
      Mechanics of the London "Fix" 102
      Gold as an Investment: Coin, Bullion, and Mining Shares . . . 107
      Are You as Smart as a French Peasant? 109
      Relative Returns from Gold and Financial Assets 110
      Misconceptions About Gold's Investment Performance 111
      Gold in Personal and Institutional Portfolios 112

  IX. **THE FUTURE OF GOLD** 113
      Can Fiat Money Be Managed Effectively? 113
      The U.S. Gold Commission 114
      Can the World Return to a Gold Standard? 114
      Can Flight from the Paper Dollar Bring Us Back to Gold? . . . 118
      The Prospects for Gold and Liberty 122

Appendix A: THE RISE AND FALL OF THE U.S. DOLLAR . 123
      Mint Ratio Altered 125
      A Unique Episode 127
      The Paper Dollar 127

Sources 131

Charts

1. World Gold Production 27
2. World Gold Stock 27
3. World Gold Production
   as a Percentage of World Gold Stock 27
4. Purchasing Power of Gold
   and of the British Pound, 1560-1994 30
5. Purchasing Power of Gold and of the U.S. Dollar, 1792-1994 .. 31
6. Federal Surplus or Deficit
   as a Percentage of GDP, 1869-1994 39
7. Annual Average Bond Yields in the United States, 1798-1994 . 77
8. Gold Held by Governments
   as a Percentage of World Gold Stock, 1913-1994 117
9. Purchasing Power of the Dollar, 1792 = 100 128
10. Purchasing Power of Gold, 1792 = 100 129

INTRODUCTION

NEARLY all the gold ever extracted from the earth in human history remains in someone's possession today, and gold continues to be mined in quantities that would have astonished the ancients. What is it that so attracts man to gold? As this book will show, gold retains its worth no matter what the economic or political situation. For this reason, among others, gold has served as money throughout human history.

Gold was first coined more than 25 centuries ago and has been used as money by all great civilizations. Greece and Rome used gold money. The industrial revolutions of Britain and America in the 18th and 19th centuries were built on a foundation of gold-convertible money. Relatively rapid and noninflationary growth was achieved in the United States, Germany, and Japan after World War II under the Bretton Woods system, which, despite serious flaws, retained gold as its centerpiece.

The political system determines whether or not gold is part of a monetary system. Historically, when there has been greater political liberty, gold has been an integral part of the monetary system. In periods of increasing government intervention in and control of economic decision-making, in war or in peace, gold has been forcibly removed from the monetary system.

A Strange New World — Without Gold Money

A quarter century has passed since the governments of the world stripped their currencies of any connection to gold. All national monies are now purely paper, backed solely by force through legal tender laws. Private money linked to gold is all but prohibited. What does it mean for man's future? The present state of money truly is unprecedented. Not since the Dark Ages has mankind seen money so pervasively subordinated to the arbitrary wishes of officials wielding a monopoly on the use of force. The economic degradation and despair of that era were sobering, given what Greece and Rome had achieved in previous centuries. In contrast, from the Renaissance until 1971, with rare and brief exceptions, money was gold or was linked to gold. And human living standards rose enormously.

Today's world is not like the Dark Ages. Neither is it the world of unprecedented political freedom and economic prosperity that existed in the 19th century. The past quarter century has seen the value of fiat paper monies gyrating beyond all expectations against one another and against gold. This period has seen bouts of price inflation and disinflation, volatile interest rates, boom and bust business cycles, and bank failures. These problems have appeared before in human history, but now they pervade our world. No nation is immune from them. What few people recognize is that each of these problems reflects in some way the abandonment of gold money.

1

Gold is a *Precious* Metal

Gold is no ordinary commodity. Over the centuries, this precious metal has served as a medium of exchange and store of wealth. Civilized people intent on bettering their condition understood that alchemy and barter would not accomplish their aims, but that sound money could. Precious metals are the basis of the only sound money known to mankind because the metals could not be created by the arbitrary whim of rulers or by the incantations of clerics. Precious metals represent tangible production. As money, they help coordinate the creation of wealth.

Those who dismiss gold as a "fetish" or a "barbarous relic," like the late British economist John Maynard Keynes, believe government-managed paper money represents a scientific advance. Gold, it is claimed, is now just another commodity. Unlike most commodities, however, very little gold is consumed. Even when fabricated into useful or decorative objects, gold usually can be recovered for resale with little effort. This is impossible for commodities such as wheat or corn, and difficult in varying degrees for other metals. More significantly, the "above ground" supply of gold that is held in a form that can be sold at moment's notice is many times (perhaps as much a 40 times) annual production. Most gold is purchased to be held, and the price of gold is little affected by vagaries of annual production or fabrication. Gold is not only a commodity: *gold is money.*

Money shorn of gold *is* an ordinary commodity — paper. Children once were taught that money does not grow on trees, that one cannot consume without first producing, that one cannot have his cake and eat it too. That ethic is consistent with gold money, but today's national monies have no fixed value. The issuers of fiat currency are driven by expedience and the funding needs of government. Central bankers and national treasury bureaucrats have set themselves up as latter-day philosopher kings, in the belief not only that their own wisdom is supreme but also, in effect, that money does grow on trees, that wealth can somehow be printed. Amidst the dross of fiat monies, however, only gold retains its value. Over the past quarter century, the paper dollar has lost more than three-fourths of its purchasing power, while that of gold has been preserved. Indeed, the purchasing power of gold has been remarkably stable for centuries. Gold's value still is widely recognized in today's markets. Whatever economists or governments say about gold, mankind still mines it, insures it, trades it, and, above all, stores it as wealth, as in centuries past. This alone is an instructive fact about gold's ageless importance.

The Modern Appeal of Gold

Even in an age of electronic banking and "information highways," it is a mistake to interpret gold as an archaic throwback, an unnecessary and

2

cumbersome deadweight in a modern and streamlined payments system. Gold and the international gold standard grew up with the industrial revolution and helped make it possible. Gold served as a credible yardstick for production and exchange, as a numeraire against which all other forms of wealth could be gauged. Far from holding back development, the gold standard lent credibility to newer developments. Checking accounts, credit cards, and electronic debits derive their value from that of the underlying monetary unit of account.

Gold should also have modern appeal in a world increasingly suspicious of central planning. The gold standard is an automatic mechanism, operated in a decentralized manner, that coordinates the self-interest of all market participants. As such, gold is uniquely equipped to accommodate the greater sophistication and complexity that come with globally integrated markets. In contrast, central banking essentially is a form of central planning, applied to the narrow but ubiquitous precincts of money and banking. Central banking is a hopeless and futile task, and its record has been very poor. No national money today serves as a reliable numeraire and no central bank can anticipate the money and credit needs of an increasingly complex marketplace. Only a system of gold-based money can do that. If men wish to throw off central planning, they will also have to throw off central banking and fiat paper money.

Gold and Economic Freedom

Gold money is inextricably linked with human freedom. Whenever men were free to choose over the centuries, they eventually settled on gold as money. As a form of money not subordinated to the arbitrary manipulations of rulers, gold permits a free economy to operate with a common denominator and standard of value. Whenever human freedom has been threatened, gold money has been attacked. That has been the pattern for most of this century, an age of nationalism, dictatorship, and the welfare state. Gold money is incompatible with statism and its extensions, such as central banking. Gold is the money that accompanies the rule of law and the sanctity of contract. If free markets are to be the basis on which humanity allocates resources, gold again will have to be the indispensable foundation of money.

This book examines the history, the economics, and the future of gold, both as money under a system of free-market capitalism, and as an investment under a system of welfare statism. It addresses basic questions about gold. Why did it become money? What did it accomplish? How and why was it replaced by government money? Why is gold now a haven from the ravages of government fiat paper money? What are gold's investment properties? What can gold tell us about the prospects of financial assets

3

denominated in fiat paper money? And what is the future of gold? Will it remain an investment haven amidst statism, or become money again, the shining beacon of a new capitalist renaissance?

I.

THE ORIGINS OF GOLD AS MONEY

PRODUCERS and traders gradually discarded barter and less suitable monetary commodities in favor of gold. They did so freely and in their own self-interest. Many of the currency units we use today, such as the dollar, the pound, and the franc, originated or evolved into specific weights of gold. Gold's value over the ages reflected objective considerations, not any intrinsic worth of the metal itself nor any subjective wishes of those who used it. Religious and governmental authorities did not bestow value of gold, but merely took advantage of the value it held for men. Gold's growing international use also coincided with the age of exploration during the Renaissance.

The Convergence on Gold

Nearly 60 countries representing the bulk of the world's economic activity participated in the international gold standard prior to World War I. This was the culmination of a long history whereby producers converged naturally on gold as a medium of exchange. How did this evolution begin?

The first use of gold as money in recorded history was in China, at the time the most advanced civilization in the world, around 1100 B.C. This money took the form of pieces of gold of a standard weight or *tael*. Eventually, coinage was developed as a seal or hallmark punched on a piece of gold to guarantee its quality or weight. The first gold coins struck in the world west of China came from Lydia around 500 B.C. Famous for its wealth and luxury, ancient Lydia was an active commercial center in the western part of Asia Minor, at the edge of the Aegean Sea. Thus a demand for money was generated. The Lydians minted their coins with electrum, a mixture of three parts gold to one part silver. Coins of pure gold were first minted under the reign of Lydia's King Croesus.

Gold and precious metals were not the first medium of exchange. When ancient civilizations first advanced beyond primitive forms of barter, they used cattle to exchange production. The word *pecuniary*, pertaining to money, is derived from the Latin, *pecus*, which means "cattle." Cattle were cumbersome because they were not easily transported or divided, and smaller items, such as seashells, came into use as money. Over the years, money has taken many forms, including iron, rare feathers, beads, and tobacco. Eventually, precious metals emerged as the preeminent form of money, especially in the most advanced civilizations. Brass, bronze, and copper were used in early coinage, but silver and gold were more extensively adopted. Various stamps of weight and fineness, together with milled and corrugated edges, were developed to guard against coin clipping and coun-

5

terfeiting. The first coinage was provided by private entrepreneurs for a profit, with the most successful delivering money of the greatest integrity.

What explains mankind's gradual convergence on gold as money? Compared to other commodities being used at various times as media of exchange, gold proved to be the most durable, divisible, portable, and homogeneous. Durability became important as wealth was increasingly stored over time. Divisibility became important as the number of transactions grew. Portability became important as trade extended geographically. Finally, homogeneity became important as various money issuers grew increasingly anonymous to money users. All of these attributes are critical to the success of any medium of exchange, and the precious metals generally tend to share them. Among the precious metals, gold is the least subject to corrosion and has the highest value per weight. Thus as production and trade grew, producers entering any market knew they could satisfy their aims best by trading their goods for gold and offering gold for the goods they ultimately sought. As gold's features became more widely recognized and gold coinage increasingly came into use, its marketability was further enhanced. Thus gold came to be used even in parts of the world where gold money had not originated.

Gold money accompanied the rise of civilization and trade. The ancient Greeks learned the use of gold coin from the Asiatics. They first minted gold coin in the 4th century B.C. in Aegina, a commercial center every bit as prosperous as Lydia had been. Gold played a lesser role in ancient Rome than it did in Asia Minor and Greece. There was some circulation of Greek gold coins in southern Italy around the 4th century. The first Roman coin, the denarius, was made of silver and struck about 268 B.C. Eventually gold superseded silver in ancient Rome in a coin called the aureus.

The decline of Western Europe into the Dark Ages was accompanied by a reversal of the earlier monetary evolution: standardized coinage was replaced in commerce by metal that was weighed, and the latter was, in turn, displaced by direct barter or no commerce at all.

Eventually, increasing contacts with the East resulted in the reintroduction of coinage into Europe. Within the century after the fall of Constantinople, coinage of gold was undertaken by several European nations and city-states. One of the earliest coins was the florin, which is said to have been minted first in Florence in 1252. However, prior to that time, and in fact for 4 centuries thereafter, silver rather than gold was the principal money-commodity used in Europe. The history of coinage throughout Europe during this period is for the most part a record of successive devaluations or debasements. For example, the English penny had been fixed at 24 grains (one pennyweight) of silver in the year 1280. This weight had been reduced to the equivalent of about 7 grains by the year 1700, even after the reminting of an abused coinage to uniform weights during 1697-98.

The English currency was one of the most stable. Countless other European currencies appeared and faded from memory. One reason for this was the widespread belief that because kings made coins, they could change them however they pleased. That the sovereign could profit by discharging his debts with coins of lightened weight may even have been viewed favorably, and not just by the sovereign, because the alternative usually was taxation. But the natural and inevitable result of each successive debasement was to make the next step in the progress toward a worthless coinage seem all the more necessary. The sovereign of course profited as a result of the increased outflow from his mint, but this was more than counteracted by the discouragement of commerce and consequent reduction of the tax base. Most of the kings and petty princes who reigned during the Middle Ages never realized that honesty with respect to the coinage was the best policy, because it was (and still is) the only policy that could succeed in the long run.

During the 300 to 400 years following the first coinage of gold florins in Florence, many of the less important transactions, and of course all of those that the decrees of the ruler could influence, were handled by counting the coins used. It was apparently customary, at least in some places, for wages to be paid by counting coins, rather than by weighing them. On the other hand, records in England indicate that all important purchases were made with the silver and gold coins being weighed and accepted as so much metal.

Beginning with the 14th century, records of commodity prices are sufficiently comprehensive to justify broad conclusions. Apparently, debasement of the coinage and devaluation were reflected fairly promptly in the domestic prices of England. Determination within close limits of the time required for such price adjustments is not practicable, but a period of from 10 to 20 years seems to have been sufficient.

This long period of devaluation and debasement ended, in the Anglo-Saxon world, around the time of the recoinage of 1697-98. This had amounted to a slight *revaluation* of British coins, or at least their standardization at a level that had prevailed several decades earlier. This recoinage was influenced by John Locke and other philosophers, who concluded that the ability of a sovereign to devalue or debase coins was an infringement on the rights of his subjects and that such powers should be eliminated along with other powers that monarchs had previously claimed by "divine right."

In 1717, the Master of the Mint, Sir Isaac Newton (yes, the same one), effectively fixed the mint price of gold at 3.89 pounds sterling per standard ounce. That weight remained unchanged (except for temporary interruptions) for more than 200 years. Over that period commodity prices in pounds sterling changed little, although they did fluctuate during the period. Not coincidentally, Britain was home to the first industrial revolution. A large part of England's economic prowess was achieved on a foundation of "hard" money.

England's fastest-growing colony also built its success with the precious metals. Colonial America at first used foreign coinage, the Spanish silver dollar being the most popular. Its first gold coins were minted and circulated in the commonwealth of Massachusetts in the 1750s. In 1787, the newly framed U.S. Constitution recognized gold and silver as standard money. The Coinage Act of 1792 authorized the minting of gold and silver coins and officially defined the dollar as specific weights of gold and silver. With the exception of the decade surrounding the Civil War, the United States employed some form of gold money for the next century. The United States enjoyed unprecedented economic growth and prosperity.

Gold as the Money of Choice

Gold money originated from the deliberate decisions of self-interested producers and traders seeking to maximize their wealth. It was not imposed by one individual, community, or government on an unsuspecting or resistant populace. Gold met genuine needs. All other media of exchange held distinct disadvantages and imposed clear obstacles at various times to the satisfaction of these needs. Thus not only did gold money evolve as the preeminent medium of exchange in the civilized world, it did so by free choice. The collective judgment of market participants proved decisive. Even when paper was developed as a convenient form of money, its value derived from its promise to pay gold, or standard money. People freely chose to use these representations of standard money.

For economists, the free choice of market participants has always been held out as a strong test of the validity of a product or device. Thus the choice of gold as money throughout history is of no small moment. As the late Austrian economist Carl Menger has written:

> Men have been led, with increasing knowledge of their individual interests, each by his own economic interests, without convention, without legal compulsion, nay, even without any regard to the common interest, to exchange goods destined for exchange (their "wares") for other goods equally destined for exchange, but more liquid.... Goods which had thus become generally accepted media of exchange were called by the Germans *Geld*, from *gelten*, i.e. to pay, to perform ... The reason why the precious metals have become the generally current medium among all peoples of advanced civilization, is because their liquidity is far and

away superior to that of all other commodities, and at the same time because they are found to be specially qualified for the concomitant and subsidiary functions of money. (Menger, 1892.)

Throughout history there have been many attempts by governments to force money on populations. Governments entered the coinage business and diluted the value of coins in order to obtain revenues. Legal tender laws, which mandate that certain monies be accepted in exchange, are another obvious example of forced money. Legal tender laws are as old as government itself. In the early stages of civilization, such laws passively tended to endorse or sanction the already widespread use of gold and other precious metals as money. In the past century, on the other hand, legal tender laws have been used to force government money on an unwilling public to the exclusion of other monies. The demise of gold money in the latter half of this century was not a result of free choice or the natural rise of more modern media of exchange. It reflected, instead, increasing government intervention in money. (See Chapter VI, "Subversion of the Gold Standard.")

Currency Units as Fixed Weights of Gold

As we have seen, gold became the money of choice through history because it served well both as a liquid medium and as a reliable store of wealth. But money also serves as a standard of value. A standard of value is like a yardstick. It is a measuring and counting device, a common denominator against which all other economic values are measured. Such a device serves a rational function in a complex, division of labor economy. Indeed, the word "rational" is derived from the Latin, *ratio*, a reckoning. Systematic measurement and counting made possible the entire field of accounting, upon which profit and loss calculations are based. A farmer who was offered ten goats for five sheep would have no idea of whether he might be better off unless he could reckon the value of both goats and sheep in terms of a common denominator, by a uniform standard of value.

The adoption of a common standard of value goes back at least as far as the adoption of a common means of payment, as far back as the history of cattle, shells, and gold as money. Just as civilization ultimately converged on gold as a medium of exchange, it also converged on gold as a standard of value. The two functions have always been closely linked. All the currencies of the world began as specific weights of precious metal. By the end of the 19th century, they were defined as specific weights of gold. Thus the drachma, the pound, the dollar, the franc, and all the other currencies of the world evolved into fixed standards of value. They were defined, by identity, as fixed weights of metal.

Some currencies were more reliable than others. Over time the world

9

converged on the most reliable ones, such as the British pound, which retained its identity as a fixed weight of silver and gold for many centuries. It was a reliable monetary yardstick. The U.S. dollar represented the same weight in gold from 1834 to 1934 and again from 1947 to 1971. These currencies were reliable to the extent their issuers, whether private or public, maintained the standard of value and delivered the promised weight of precious metals on demand. The credibility of that commitment, not the supply and demand of the specific currencies as such, determined the value of money. The more credible the standard, the more the supply of money would be demanded. Currencies of lesser credibility could attract little demand, regardless of supply. (See Chapter III, "The Gold Standard in Theory.")

Gold as an Objective Value

The long-evolved convergence on gold has an objective basis in fact. On the one hand, producers and traders have exhibited specific needs for a medium of exchange, a store of wealth, and a standard of value. On the other hand, the actual physical attributes of the precious metals, especially of gold, have satisfied those needs better than any other commodity or device. Thus, gold's value is objective.

This is in contrast to two opposing, but misguided, accounts of gold's value. One argues that gold possesses intrinsic value, or value in and of itself, apart from any value estimates on the part of its users. Another argues that money in general (and gold in particular when it circulated as money) is a subjective value, a mere social convention agreed to by its users, regardless of its specific attributes. Thus it is said that gold is passe today because no one agrees to use it as money, and that those who still do appreciate gold must do so because they believe it is imbued with some intrinsic worth (Frankel, 1977).

There is no basis for these theories either in history or in fact. Gold is not itself wealth and has no direct capacity by itself to satisfy even the most basic of human needs. On a deserted island, one is much better off finding fruit-laden trees than gold-laden streams. Nor is social agreement by itself sufficient to engender reliable money. Money is not merely anything we happen to say it is, simply because we say it. The fiat paper monies of today are a case in point. They are issued for the most part by democratically elected governments, but they represent arbitrary and unreliable standards. As such, they generally are unfit to serve as money. Accordingly, they have all depreciated against gold. The *form* in which money is held must always serve the *function* of money. Thus money in the form of gold has always tended to represent a unified and integrated standard of objective value.

10

The Alleged "Mystical Qualities" of Gold

Some monetary historians attribute mystical qualities to gold and minimize the objective basis for its adoption. They attempt to convert mankind's rational estimate of gold's value into a perverse fetish:

> To grasp the frame of mind which produced such beliefs as the fetishism of gold, we must turn back through the centuries to a mentality which has now become foreign and strange to us. We must imagine a magical world view in which astrology existed rather than astronomy, alchemy rather than chemistry, and number mysticism rather than mathematics. The belief in imitative and contagious magic exists in all primitive cultures, and ancient Greek and Rome were suffused with such ideas and practices. (Desmonde, 1962, p. 81.)

Modern critics of gold have built on this historical misinterpretation (Einzig, 1949).

In part these errors stem from the fact that gold was chosen as money very early in mankind's history. Thus it often is believed that history involves an unbroken progression upward, from the more primitive to the more advanced. But this is a profound mistake. While the Greek and Roman civilizations retained mystical influences from an earlier age, those civilizations are best characterized for their break with a mystical past. They embraced reason and logic, more democratic forms of government, and the rule of law. They adopted gold money to circulate trade.

Mankind's history is not a constant progression. Consider the fall of Greco-Roman civilization and the subsequent centuries of intellectual darkness and economic stagnation. There was little reason to use gold money in such times. The love of money and material comfort were considered the root of all evil by the church. Only during the Renaissance and the Enlightenment, with the rebirth of reason and science, did economic growth, trade, and the use of gold money flourish once again. The emergence of totalitarian governments and the dominance of the welfare state for most of this century, following a century of relative peace and prosperity after the Napoleonic Wars, offers yet another example of retrogression. Not coincidentally, in the current century gold has been banished from the world monetary system.

A particularly perverse interpretation of gold's value came from its most famous critic, the late British economist John Maynard Keynes, who attributed man's desire for the precious metal not to reason or facts but to deep, dark Freudian obsessions (Skidelsky, 1994, pp. 88, 188, 234). Keynes endorsed Freud's claim, for example, that the hoarding of gold reflected "anal-retentive" behavior. His solution to such hoarding was to rid childish man of his filthy gold by replacing it with government money.

11

There is nothing magical, mystical or obsessive about gold. Nor was gold ever imposed on men against their will by the state. On the contrary, as gold's real value became widely recognized in more rational and advanced eras, gold was always prone to being co-opted by church and state alike. These two institutions never imbued gold with a value it did not already possess. If anything, they have been enemies of gold through the ages, denouncing it as evil or seizing it for its alleged evil consequences.

Gold and Exploration

Gold was not sought because it created wealth, but because it represented wealth. The pursuit of gold symbolized a pursuit of the economic freedom that gave gold its value. Money and gold have always been in demand whenever economic activity and trade flourished. Cultures with little such activity tend not to attract money. For money to be used, there must already exist multilateral exchange between products. This occurs most extensively in advanced, division of labor economies. Monetary historian Pierre Vilar has described the process during the Renaissance:

> If an influx of gold is to have a profound economic meaning, there must be a profound economic reason for it; it must correspond to an upsurge in exchange and in production, and cannot result simply from enrichment through war.... Gold came back to Europe, in fact, when there was a trade surplus to attract it, or more simply, when Europe began selling more than it bought.... The triumph of the commercial cities, especially those around the Mediterranean, was formalized in the adoption of internationally accepted gold coin.... The minting of gold was therefore a consequence of Western economic development and not a cause (even though there is always some inter-action).... Trade created money rather than money trade. (Vilar, 1991, pp. 27, 34-36.)

Vilar shows that gold exploration was a rational response to basic economic pressures. The increase in production and population during the Renaissance, and in periods of economic expansion ever since, tended to bring about a fall in prices relative to gold. The upward valuation of gold relative to other things made gold much sought after. When gold was discovered, prices stabilized or increased. The initial impetus for gold discoveries always was economic growth and the rise of commercial trade.

Modern economists have tended to reverse this established order of events, believing that money creates wealth, not the other way around. During the economic depression of the 1930s, Keynes argued that inflation and monetary devaluations could stimulate trade and foster recovery. In doing so he also speculated about the possibility of rewriting monetary history in order to support his theories:

> It would be a fascinating task to rewrite Economic History, in light of

these ideas, from its remote beginnings; to conjecture whether the civilizations of Sumeria and Egypt drew their stimulus from the gold of Arabia … whether the greatness of Athens depended on the silver of Laurium … how far the dispersal by Alexander of the bank reserves of Persia was responsible for the outburst of economic progress in the Mediterranean basin, of which Rome ultimately succeeded to reap the fruits … whether it was a coincidence that the decline and fall of Rome was contemporaneous with the most prolonged and drastic deflation … and whether the long stagnation of the Middle Ages might not have been more surely caused by Europe's meager supply of the monetary metals than by monasticism or Gothic frenzy. (Keynes, 1930, Volume II, p. 150.)

History aside, Keynes would claim in the 1930s that the abolition of gold and the creation of unlimited amounts of paper money would foster economic development. He had a fetish for paper money verging on alchemy. Today, this Keynesian "experiment" is recognized by most economists as futile and illusory. Inflating does not create wealth; it destroys it. (See Chapter VII, "Central Banking and Gold.") Attempts by Keynes to rewrite history on the basis of false theories have proved no less illusory. Yet as Vilar notes, many people still tend to believe in the illusion:

The 20th century now believes that everything will be different if only we can increase or decrease the supply of money or can expand and contract credit. It is dangerous to make this kind of simplified analysis, either in interpreting history or in monetary matters. The real problem is the extent of man's freedom vis-à-vis what he has created. (Vilar, 1991, p. 8.)

Whenever in history men were left free to create, they created material abundance. And they used gold money to help do so. There is great symbolism in the fact that every gold coin ever struck in America has contained the word "liberty." Whenever mysticism or secular statism reigned, prosperity and gold were submerged. Through the ages, in monetary matters, free men proclaimed "in gold we trust." This is in sharp contrast to the motto "in God we trust" that our Government now proclaims on its paper money. Gold and liberty are inextricably linked. The reduced role of gold in our current monetary system may be seen as a reflection of our reduced freedom, compared to past eras.

II.

FREE BANKING AND GOLD

IN modern times the production of coins and currency is everywhere a monopoly of the state. Laws against counterfeiting government money are intended to preserve this exclusive function. Private banks still create deposits convertible into standard money, but they are no longer allowed to provide standard money. Needless to say, this government monopoly has not delivered money of high quality. In earlier times entrepreneurs provided money through private mints and banks. In contrast to the low-quality government money of today, private money was sound and served as a solid foundation for long-term economic growth.

Private Mints, Money Changers, and Goldsmiths

As men converged on gold as money it was natural that they also sought reliable and convenient forms of coinage, of storing coins, and of exchanging them. The first coins were minted by private individuals and goldsmiths. Private mints evolved to guarantee the weight and fineness of coins. This permitted traders to overcome the trouble of weighing or assaying bits of gold or disparate coins in every transaction. Gradually, unbranded bits of metal were less accepted and gave way to coins of a guaranteed standard. Denominations reflected the needs of trade. People began to use the coins of private minters with the highest reputations for delivering good quality money. Private coins have flourished many times in history, including a period of more than 3 decades before the U.S. Civil War (Barnard, 1916-17). According to one history of U.S. experience with private coinage,

> Gold coiners were businessmen who saw a profit for themselves in providing what was only incidentally an essential economic service. The mint operators not only provided an alternate coinage, but also a means of converting gold into currency. This promoted immigration into a region and a growing need for more coinage . . . The private mints made possible the development of their regions and the nation at large. (Kagin, 1981.)

Economic development increases the number and variety of transactions requiring money. There are incentives to lower transaction costs by standardizing money. Private mints helped achieve this result.

Unfortunately, from ancient times private mints frequently were co-opted by governments, not to guarantee better money, but to obtain money not otherwise available through taxing or borrowing. Governments periodically debased money at their own mints by clipping gold from coins or by partially substituting baser metals for gold. Today such monetary debasement finds its equivalent in inflating — the creation of excess purchasing media. Any mint will charge a small fee for converting bullion into coins. When this is done by an official mint the charge is called "seignorage." If this charge was in excess of mint expenses, it became a major source of state revenue, while simultaneously contributing to the circulation of bad money. The decline of the Roman Empire was accompanied by such a debasement, not by a "deflation" as Keynes had once surmised.

Besides private minters, money changers played a key role in the early development of banking. They offered to buy and sell local and foreign coins, earning commissions in the process. The word "bank" itself is derived from the medieval Latin *bancus*, which originally referred to the bench or stall where a tradesman sat, and came to refer to the table or counter where money changers conducted their business. Initially, traders had to count out specific amounts of coin and transport them to and from money changers. These costs were reduced when traders established standing account balances with the money changers, which were built up and drawn down as needed. Eventually, because traders often frequented the same money changers, it proved more efficient to make transfers of coin at the money changer's place of business and to do so by making book transfers instead of physically moving the coin. Thus, money changers began to take on warehousing and safekeeping functions. Money changers had existed in Greece and Rome, but the first modern references to banking of this sort date back to the 12th and 13th centuries, the beginning of the Renaissance, in Italian cities like Genoa, then the most advanced part of Europe (de Roover, 1974).

Aside from the money changers, some of the earliest known banks were goldsmiths and mintmasters, appearing in 17th-century England. At first they provided strictly warehouse facilities for fees. Wealthy depositors began to lodge a considerable portion of their precious metals with the most reputable vault owners. They received warehouse receipts as evidence of their deposits. Gradually, as these receipts earned a reputation for soundness, they circulated as money, just as readily as coin. Private goldsmiths operating as banks successfully reduced the cost and raised the efficiency of using the precious metals as money. They developed basic money-transfer services to minimize the physical handling of coin, as did the money changers.

In every community where banking flourished, it promoted a gradual substitution of gold deposit receipts for gold itself. Representative money took its place aside standard money. Adam Smith observed the economic advantages of this development in his book, *The Wealth of Nations*:

> The substitution of paper in the room of gold and silver money, replaces
> a very expensive instrument of commerce with one much less costly, and

16

sometimes equally convenient. Circulation comes to be carried on by a new wheel, which it costs less both to erect and to maintain than the old one.... When the people of any particular country have such confidence in the fortune, probity, and prudence of a particular banker, as to believe that he is always ready to pay upon demand such of his promissory notes as are likely to be at any time presented to him, those notes come to have the same currency as gold and silver money, from the confidence that such money can at any time be had for them. (Smith, 1776, pp. 276-277.)

Despite the introduction of paper claims on gold, gold remained as standard money under free banking. Gold was the asset on which currency was a claim. Precious metal coins continued to circulate alongside paper currency and checks, but the value of these claims rested solely on the credibility of private banks to meet redemptions on demand. As Adam Smith pointed out, free banking operates best when based on the precious metals:

The judicious operations of banking, by providing, if I may be allowed so violent a metaphor, a sort of wagon-way through the air, enable the country to convert, as it were, a great part of its highways into good pastures and cornfields, and thereby to increase very considerably the annual produce of its land and labor. The commerce and industry of the country, however, it must be acknowledged, though they may be some-what augmented, cannot be altogether so secure when they are thus, as it were, suspended upon the Daedalian wings of paper money as when they travel about upon the solid ground of gold and silver. (Smith, 1776, p. 305.)

Smith recognized that the wealth of nations was built upon sound money and that sound money consisted of gold and silver and convertible bank notes.

The Evolution of Free Banking

The simple gold-transfer services provided by money changers and goldsmiths involved no intermediation between borrowers and savers. The strict warehouse bankers lent out none of their depositors' gold and earned no interest. Legally, they were a bailee, not a debtor to depositors. Loans were made only out of a banker's personal wealth, but, as with coinage, the gains made possible by exhibiting a sound reputation brought with it high-quality private banking. Revenues for a strict warehouse bank were limited to the fees paid by depositors for safekeeping services. Gold and other precious metal deposits related one-for-one to customer claims on them.

As commercial trade expanded and the wealth of depositors grew, two factors contributed to a natural evolution favoring "fractional reserve"

17

banking. Commercial traders sought loans from banks while depositors sought ways to minimize the expense associated with storing specie at banks. Meanwhile, banks realized they could lend specie at interest and in turn could promise to pay depositors some part of that interest to compensate for the risk of patronizing a fractional reserve bank. Instead of paying storage fees, depositors would receive interest income. Gold and other specie deposits were uniform in quality and fungible, so there was no obstacle to using them interchangeably. The risk of fractional reserves was that a bank might lend too much specie relative to the claims upon it, or, because loans were increasingly made by creating claims (currency and checks), to create too many.

The art of sound commercial banking involved managing the balance between earning interest income on loans and paying interest expense on deposits, while still meeting periodic specie withdrawals on demand. Banks could count on "the law of large numbers," the principle that not *all* depositors would withdraw *all* their money *all* at once. This law held true only for sound banks, however. The alternative to the law of large numbers — a "run" on a bank by all depositors at once — was a threat that encouraged bankers to be prudent.

Lending practices under free banking were prudent. To enhance liquidity under fractional reserves, banks made only short-term self-liquidating commercial loans. This policy, known as the "real-bills" doctrine, meant the advancing of loans only against real bills of exchange evidencing definite trade between enterprises. For each bank individually, this doctrine maximized liquidity as well as profitability, since loans against real bills tended to have lower default rates. In aggregate, the doctrine meant that to the extent representative money was issued in excess of gold deposits, it was issued against real economic output, and thus would not contribute to inflation.

The profit motive was consistent with sound private banking and price stability in other ways. To maximize profits, private banks had to be careful not to issue too many claims on gold deposits, which involved costs not only in the form of interest expense but also in risking inconvertibility and closure. These costs further discouraged private banks from inflating. In addition to the threat of bank runs by depositors, banks faced disciplinary competition from each other. Competitive currency issuance meant that banks often were in possession of each others' notes, a natural result of taking deposits for customers in both gold and currency. Banks presented these notes to one another for redemption, since they were of no use to them otherwise. There evolved a system of clearinghouses to make these note exchanges more efficient and to settle only the net differences in gold at the end of each day. Member banks that issued too many claims (currency and checks) on their gold reserves relative to the claims issued by competitors faced an adverse clearing and lost gold. Thus effective disciplines against overissuance evolved naturally.

The rise of fractional reserve banking benefited borrowers, bankers, and depositors alike. However, it altered the original relationship between banks and depositors in an important way. Instead of playing the role of bailee issuing receipts in its sole capacity as a warehouse, banks now were debtors issuing promissory notes, or bank notes, to depositors in their capacity as risk-taking intermediaries. Fee-based safekeeping services continued to be provided (and still are today), but over time these tended to diminish as a share of total bank income. From the time fractional reserves were first instituted, the art of commercial banking began to hold sway. As long as a bank's currency and demand deposits were convertible and its loans liquid, it could attract profitable business without in any way endangering the larger monetary system in the process. Gold was the anchor that secured fractional reserve banking.

Free banking is characterized by privately owned banks and clearinghouses, the issuance of specie-convertible currency, decentralized reserves, commercial lending guided by the "real-bills" doctrine, and the absence of legal restrictions. Free banks are properly subject to the general legal prohibition against fraud or breach of contract, but otherwise they are left free from government controls or interventions of any kind. Free banking contrasts sharply with its antithesis, central banking, a government-imposed system that has ruled for most of this century. (See Chapter VII, "Central Banking and Gold.") Under free banking there is no central bank or "monetary policy," no centralization of reserves or government hoarding of gold, no legal monopoly on currency or legal tender laws, no official lender of last resort, bailouts, reserve requirements, lending or branching rules, usury laws, state credit agencies, or deposit insurance.

With one minor exception pertaining to small-denomination bank notes, which he feared might not be continually redeemed at banks, Adam Smith endorsed complete free banking:

> If bankers are restrained from issuing any circulating bank notes, or notes payable to the bearer for less than a certain sum; and if they are subject to the obligation of an immediate and unconditional payment of such bank notes as soon as presented, their trade may, with safety to the public, be rendered in all respects perfectly free. (Smith, 1776, p. 313.)

Smith was careful to stress the legal importance of government enforcing money contracts. The ideas of Smith and his followers guided government policy toward banking for most of the 19th century. Thus as commercial banking continued to evolve, it was left predominantly free of government intervention. This made it possible for banking to expand safely with the needs of trade.

Free Banking and Economic Development

Far from being an impediment to this progress, free banking helped contribute to it. Free banking delivered relatively stable prices for most of the 19th century, no doubt a consequence of issuing bank notes and checking accounts convertible into gold and silver. This stability was occasionally disrupted by government-sanctioned suspensions of convertibility during wartime. But some of the most expansive and sustained periods of economic growth in world history, primarily during the 19th century, occurred under systems of free banking and gold. Stable money fostered economic calculation and long-range planning. Sound lending practices were commonplace. There was no reckless hunt for marginally creditworthy borrowers. Free banks financed the most productive enterprises and rewarded the most prudent savers.

Like all middlemen, bankers provided more attractive terms to the ultimate transactors between whom they mediated than those transactors could have obtained otherwise. By distinguishing between good and bad risks and pooling the good ones, banks bore less risk than ultimate lenders would have by lending directly to ultimate borrowers. In so doing, they increased total lending and reduced interest rates to borrowers. And by offering a low-risk way for savers to earn a return on their funds, banks attracted funds that would otherwise have lain idle. Banks thus increased the amount, and above all, the quality of saving and investment, thereby speeding up economic development. It is no exaggeration to say that banks converted the holder of money from a miser who diverted costly resources from competing uses to a supplier of the capital that fueled economic growth (Glasner, 1989, p. 13).

But it was not banking alone that helped deliver the economic achievements of the 19th century. After all, the banking systems of the 20th century have coincided with relatively subpar economic performance. They have been highly regulated systems operating under the thumb of central bankers. Gold-based free banking, on the other hand, was critical to the economic success of the 19th century. There are good reasons for the difference in economic performance between the 2 centuries:

> The aggregate performance of an economy on a gold standard is likely to be better under free banking than under central banking. A large body of theoretical and historical work in economics identifies errors in money supply as a significant source of business cycle disturbances. The advantage of free banking is that a large number of issuers minimizes the chances for large-scale errors in the money supply. One reason is readily appar-

ent: No single issuer controls a large share of the circulation. Equally important, the multiplicity of issuers brings with it, in the form of the interbank clearinghouse for bank notes and checks, an automatic mechanism for preventing major money supply errors by any single bank. The clearinghouse gives each issuer both the information to detect, and the incentive to correct promptly, any deviation of the quantity of currency and checks it supplies from the quantity that the public desires to hold. This process of negative feedback is absent from a central banking system, where the supply of bank notes is monopolized and the liabilities of the central bank are held as reserves by commercial banks. Only with free banking is the operation of the gold standard fully self-regulating. (White, 1989, pp. 157-158.)

Free banking and the gold standard grew up together historically and were inextricably linked in practice. Out of a convergence on gold money came time-tested free banking techniques.

Free Banking in History

Free banking did not develop overnight, nor was it imposed legislatively. It evolved over many centuries by the free choice and self-interest of money users, depositors, bankers, and borrowers alike. A precondition for its growth was the return of freedom and economic activity during the Renaissance. But free banking achieved its greatest success in the Western world during the 18th and 19th centuries, when the world converged on gold money to the widest extent ever. Even in today's highly regulated period, the better experiences in banking are due to the freer elements that remain.

Banking has never been fully free of government interference. Even in its infancy during the Renaissance it faced obstacles imposed by both church and state. The money changers were condemned as evil thieves. Religious opposition to the lending of money and the charging of interest were translated into usury laws. Governments periodically confiscated gold from conveniently concentrated sources such as mints. Legal tender laws and interventions in minting alternately favored silver or gold at various times. Whenever governments did intervene in minting they invariably debased the coinage. Only when the rule of law and constitutional government became more widespread during the Enlightenment did banking become progressively more free.

There have been about 60 free banking systems in world history, lasting from just a few years to more than a century (Dowd, 1992, pp. 7-47). The high point for free banking was the 18th and 19th centuries in the Western world. The longest and most notable episodes include Scotland (1716-1845), Canada (1817-1914), Sweden (1831-1901), Switzerland (1834-1907), and the United States (1834-1914). In 1837, a year after President Andrew Jackson vetoed the rechartering of the Bank of the United States, helping to usher in American free banking, he wrote the following to a friend:

> Now is the time to separate the government from all banks. Receive and disburse the revenue in nothing but gold and silver coin, and the circulation of our coin through all public disbursements will regulate the currency forever hereafter. Keep the government free from all embarrassments, whilst it leaves the commercial community to trade upon its own capital, and the banks to accommodate it with such exchange and credit as best suits their interests — both being money making concerns, devoid of patriotism, looking alone to their interests — regardless of all others. It has been, and ever will be a curse to the government to have any entanglement or interest with either, more than a general superintending care of all. (Quoted in Hammond, 1947, p. 12.)

This reasoned and principled defense of laissez-faire banking by a sitting American president would be unheard of in the 20th century, when intervention has been rampant. Yet it was Andrew Jackson's conception of money and banking that guided America's economic ascendance in the 19th century.

Free banking systems have displayed many positive features. Each historical episode involved economically sophisticated countries becoming increasingly more industrialized. Free banking systems fueled no reckless inflations, credit expansions, or panics. They exhibited no tendency toward a concentration of currency issuance in a single bank. All free banking systems, even smaller ones, had more than one note-issuing bank. Most had multiple issuers. Yet free bank currencies were defined in terms of a common standard of value, the fixed weights of gold that units of account such as the dollar represented. By honing to that standard, free banks attracted customers. Free banks also maintained exchange rate stability and a smoothly functioning classical gold standard:

> Free banking systems maintained exchange rate stability by giving people the right to convert bank notes and deposits into gold or silver at a fixed rate.... The commercial customs and the legal framework of the 19th century made free banking inherently a regime of convertibility. Free banking had strong competitive incentives to maintain convertibility as a way of attracting customers. Except when governments allowed banks to renege on their previous contractual obligations of convertibility, there seems to have been no cases of free banking systems issuing fiat-money liabilities carrying no promise of fixed-rate convertibility.... Free banking's success at maintaining peacetime convertibility ... suggests that free banking was what enabled the gold standard to persist before World War I. (Schuler, 1992, pp. 20-21.)

History confirms that the successes achieved by other industries when they are free of government interference are no less achievable in money and banking. Free banking flourished during the heyday of the international gold coin standard in the 19th century. That system was abandoned forever during World War I. But free banking episodes came to an end, not because they failed, but because governments sought ways to finance their burgeoning operations by co-opting private money and banking systems. Central banking would prove inimical to gold money. (See Chapter VI, "Subversion of the Gold Standard.")

Myths About Free Banking

Despite the documented successes of free banking systems in history, a number of myths persist about the performance of laissez-faire banking. It is argued that numerous competing free bank currencies proved confusing, that fraud was rampant, that free banks were prone to inflating, that "wildcat banking" and "money panics" and boom-bust cycles proliferated and were inherent in systems of free banking. These misconceptions stem from the fact that free banking systems were predominantly free but not fully so. Problems such as proliferating note issues, counterfeiting and fraud, suspensions of convertibility, price inflation, and boom-bust cycles were never chronic under free banking. When they did occur they proved to be a consequence of government legal restrictions.

There was no problem with the variety of free bank currencies, since they were all defined in terms of a common money, gold. Problems of proliferation arose only when government restrictions on branching artificially increased the number of banks, especially in the United States. Similarly, counterfeiting and fraudulent note issue were not serious problems under free banking. Even where such activity at first seemed widespread — on the U.S. frontier before the Civil War by the so-called "wildcat" banks — subsequent research has found the episodes to be exaggerated and nonetheless fostered by state intervention (Rockoff, 1975, pp. 13-33). These episodes arose directly in consequence of the bond collateral restrictions on private currency. Financially weak frontier states forced banks to buy state bonds as bank note collateral, ostensibly to secure the notes, but primarily as a means of obtaining funds not available by taxing. As state bond values fell, so did these banks, but not before enriching fly-by-night operators and fleecing unsuspecting depositors. Government also failed to punish suspensions of convertibility, because in doing so it freed banks from having to call in payment on government loans. The fault for related problems clearly lies with government, not with free markets.

In the same vein, the high prices of the Civil War and its aftermath resulted from government issued pure paper "greenbacks," not from the

California gold discoveries more than a decade earlier nor from any inherent inflationary tendency of free banking. And the intermittent "money panics" of the late-19th century, a source of complaints about an "inelastic currency" and the root of many calls for a single government currency and the Federal Reserve (formed in 1914), were also a consequence of bank note collateral regulations. A declining national debt limited the supply of bonds required to secure bank currency, precisely when economic activity and the demand for money to circulate it were expanding. All the ills popularly ascribed to free banking in history are a result not of freedom, but of government interventions that tended to disrupt a self-regulating system.

As mentioned, free banking systems did not fail on their own. They were gradually undermined and superseded by government-sponsored central banking. The first central bank, the Bank of England, was established in 1694 to finance a war with France. In the United States, the Federal Government assumed many monetary functions during the Civil War, even though it did not establish a central bank until 50 years later. The Federal Reserve was established in 1914 during the "progressive era," when government powers were being concentrated and expanded in many other ways as well, such as the anti-trust laws and the national income tax. The German central bank was established in 1875 and grew in size precisely when Bismarck began building the first full-scale welfare state. Most of today's major central banks — those in the United States, Germany, Switzerland, Japan, Italy, and Canada, for example, were established in the 50 years or so around the turn of the century, when nationalism and interventionism were on the rise (see Chapter VI, "Subversion of the Gold Standard," and Chapter VII, "Central Banking and Gold"). The suspension of gold convertibility during War World I and the rise of central banking put an end to otherwise successful systems of free banking based on gold money.

III.

THE GOLD STANDARD IN THEORY

THAT widespread use of gold as standard money made possible a vast expansion of economic activity was due to gold's relative stability as a standard of value. Such stability was, and is, an indispensable precondition for business calculation and planning. Adam Smith, David Ricardo, and other economists of the Classical School of the late 18th and early 19th centuries were the first to describe and study economic activity in a scientific way. They identified general principles, including those pertaining to the use of gold and money. The theories about the operation of the gold standard first offered by the Classical economists still are discussed and debated, but now with the added benefit of hindsight and over 2 centuries of monetary experience since Smith.

A Standard of Value

We have seen why men converged on gold as money over the centuries and why, since the Renaissance and the vast expansion of trade, they also developed convenient representations of gold, such as bank notes and checking deposits. As economic activity expanded, gold's importance as a standard of value outpaced its role as a medium of exchange. Paper claims increasingly were used as such media, in place of gold and specie, but these claims were issued against a standard.

As discussed earlier, a standard of value is a measuring device, like a yardstick. Money in this sense is a common denominator against which all other economic values are reckoned. The key feature of a standard of value is that it remains fixed. Thus, the primary value of a yardstick is that it remains forever equal to three feet. The supply and demand for yardsticks as such do not alter the identity that yardsticks represent: a yard *is* three feet. So with money. Fluctuations in any standard of value only nullify its *raison d'etre*. In fact, it is the integrity of the standard of value itself that determines the supply and demand for it. Reliable yardsticks are more readily supplied and demanded than unreliable ones. Throughout history, gold has been the most reliable monetary yardstick known.

A gold standard means that economic goods and services are valued in relation to specific weights of gold, weights that comprise the various units of account that evolved over time, such as the dollar, the pound, the mark, or the franc. Paper claims on gold, denominated in dollars or other units of account, retain their value in the marketplace only to the extent they are freely convertible into fixed weights of gold. They are claims in the strictest sense — direct claims on gold — and valuable only to the extent currency issuers are credible and meet such claims whenever presented. As discussed below, the fact that gold possesses a relatively stable purchasing power makes it uniquely fitted to serve as a monetary standard of value.

Like No Other Commodity

As history shows, gold is no ordinary commodity. Most commodities are produced for purposes of consumption. Agricultural products, energy, even steel and aluminum are all produced for consumption. Gold is different. Gold is produced for the purpose of accumulation. Most of the gold taken from the ground throughout man's history — a stock now totaling in excess of three and a half billion ounces — still exists aboveground (see Chart 2). Very little of this gold is used in ways that preclude its eventual recovery. The fraction of the gold supply used for ornamentation and jewelry is relatively small and much of it is in high-carat ("Asian") jewelry, in which the value added in fabrication is quite low in relation to the value of the metal. Such jewelry is held as a form of savings.

Very little gold has been lost over the years, because of its high value and ease of its retrieval and refabrication relative to other commodities. Throughout history gold has been a store of wealth and a standard of value, regardless of whether it was used as a medium of exchange. Even today, when government paper currency by law must be used as the medium of exchange, gold still is accumulated as wealth.

That fact that gold is accumulated, not consumed, is important to the evolution and operation of a gold standard. The increments to the aboveground stock of gold are but a very small fraction of that stock. In this century, the average annual increment to the aboveground stock of gold coming out of the mines has been approximately 2 percent (see Chart 1 and Chart 3). This is in marked contrast to consumed commodities, whose annual production often is a very high fraction, if not a multiple, of available stocks at any point in time. As a result, gold's real value — what it will purchase in goods and services — is the least variable of any commodity. The late Roy Jastram, a professor of economics at Berkeley, once referred to this tendency for gold's real value to be stable as "the golden constant" (Jastram, 1977).

The Golden Constant

The value of any economic good is determined by supply and demand, at any point in time. That principle applies as much to gold as to other commodities. But since the relevant supply of gold is the vast aboveground stock that has been accumulated through the ages, not the annual increment to that stock, changes in supply play a relatively insignificant role in determining gold's price. This is not to say that the value of gold does not fluctuate in relation to other things. Even during the operation of the clas-

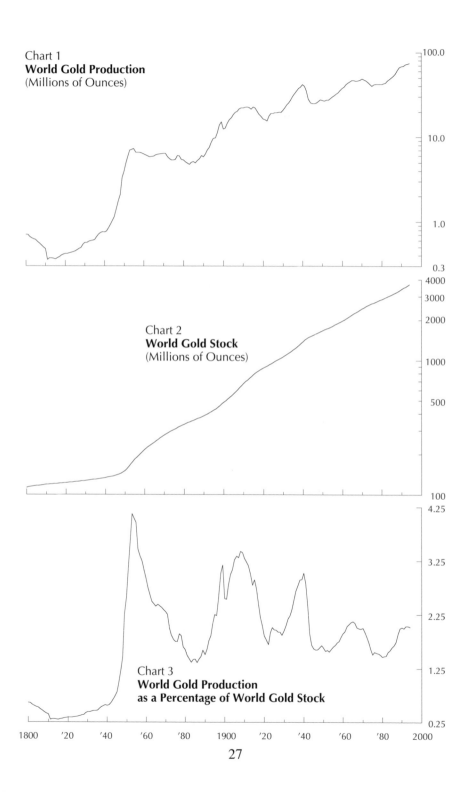

Chart 1
World Gold Production
(Millions of Ounces)

100.0

10.0

1.0

0.3

Chart 2
World Gold Stock
(Millions of Ounces)

4000
3000

2000

1000

500

100

4.25

3.25

2.25

Chart 3
**World Gold Production
as a Percentage of World Gold Stock**

1.25

0.25

1800   '20   '40   '60   '80   1900   '20   '40   '60   '80   2000

27

sical gold standard, a given amount of gold could be exchanged for more at some times than at others. Still, the cost of living fluctuated in a fairly narrow range.*

In Chapter I, we indicated how trade and commerce can bring gold to regions and countries where it is not mined. Gold flows to regions and countries where it has a high value, because prices are low, and out of areas where its value is low and prices are high. Such flows tend to equalize prices globally. If the equilibrium price level is low, gold mining will be encouraged and *vice versa*. The California and Klondike gold rushes, to name just two examples, were not historical accidents — it was the low prices and high purchasing power of gold during the 1840s and 1890s that prompted men to go to (what were, at the time) the ends of the earth in search of gold. In short, even though the supply of gold from mines is a minor factor in the market, such supplies tend to fluctuate in a fashion that tends to stabilize the purchasing power of gold.

What about the demand for gold? We have seen through the ages, even up to the present time, that gold has always been in demand as a medium of exchange and store of wealth. The fact that gold is no longer used extensively as a medium of exchange is due to legal tender laws that compel the use of government paper currency (see Chapter V, "Political and Legal Issues"). Thus the demand for gold also has been relatively stable over the centuries, even though the demand for gold has risen during periods of distrust in fiat paper monies.

The combined effect of a relatively stable supply and demand for gold has been that gold's real value has remained relatively constant over time. Indeed, this is an important reason men converged on gold as money. While there are no monetary standards absolutely fixed in value for all time, gold has come the closest. Aside from the crucial fact that gold did indeed become the money of choice, empirical support for the "golden constant" is extensive. Jastram (1977) analyzed more than 4 centuries of gold and price data from Great Britain and the United States in order to measure gold's real purchasing power. He obtained a consistent price series for gold as well as for other commodities, denominated in pounds

---

* Price data for the United States suggest that the range of such fluctuations might be as large as 3 (*i.e.*, that even when the dollar was freely convertible into gold, it could at some times purchase three times as much as it could at others). This is markedly less than the potential range (infinity) for paper currency that can become worthless. However, the price indexes used to compute this 3 to 1 range were derived long after the fact and were based on commodity price quotations published in newspapers, mainly in port cities such as New York or New Orleans. These prices were subject to the most extreme fluctuations of crop and business cycles, including those of our trading partners. It is virtually certain that the "cost of living" fluctuated within a much narrower range.

and dollars. He divided the commodity price series by the gold price series, to obtain the real price of gold, or what gold would buy in terms of other commodities.

Remarkably, Jastram found that gold's purchasing power was relatively constant through more than 4 centuries (see Chart 4). For most of this history, Britain and the United States were on a gold standard. The pound and the dollar were defined in terms of a fixed weight of gold, which meant that the price of gold was fixed. Commodity prices also tended to be stable, and the real value of gold also was quite stable over long periods of time. Even during episodes when the gold standard was suspended and price inflation took hold, gold still retained its relatively constant purchasing power. When prices rose due to inflating, so did gold prices. If prices eventually fell, so did the price of gold. In either instance, a certain weight in gold bought substantially the same basket of commodities. Jastram found that gold's real purchasing power was less stable in the short run than in the long run. But short-term instability in gold's real value tended to occur most when currencies were unhinged from gold and there was great uncertainty about their value.

There are everyday examples that illustrate the "golden constant." In the 1930s, an ounce of gold ($35 per ounce) bought a good man's suit. That is the situation today: even though the price of a suit now is more than ten times as high, so is the price of gold. Before OPEC became a household word in 1973, an ounce of gold bought about 20 barrels of oil ($1.75 per barrel). Today an ounce of gold still buys about 20 barrels of oil, even though the price of oil now is more than ten times higher. Which monetary values have changed over these years? Not gold, whose real purchasing power has been relatively constant. What has changed — for the worse — has been the purchasing power of the paper dollar. Not only has the dollar's (and other currencies') purchasing power fallen, it has fallen most in the decades when it has been unhinged from gold.

A market economy requires a dependable monetary yardstick not subject to arbitrary manipulation. A government-operated system of central banking is ill-equipped to provide such a yardstick. On both theoretical and historical grounds, central banking is incompatible with gold money (see Chapter VII, "Central Banking and Gold"). The fact that of all commodities the purchasing power of gold is the most stable in real value, makes a gold standard the preeminent market-oriented monetary system. Since standard money under a gold standard is gold, what principles guide its production? What are the economics of gold mining? Is mining a sound base for money? What are the effects of a gold standard on prices, business cycles, and long-term rates of economic growth? How does government, with no power over money, finance its operations under such a system?

29

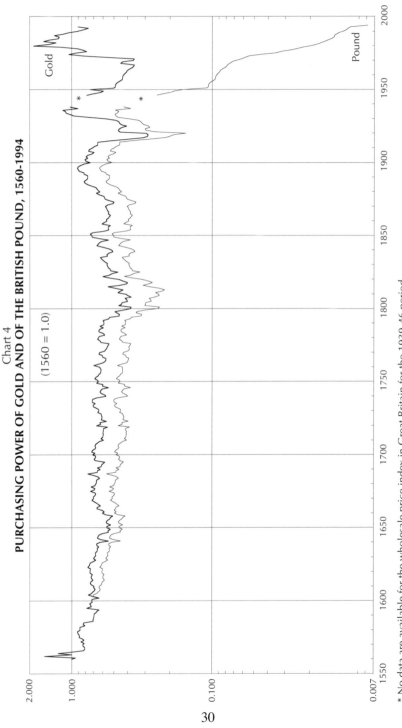

Chart 4
PURCHASING POWER OF GOLD AND OF THE BRITISH POUND, 1560-1994

(1560 = 1.0)

Gold

Pound

* No data are available for the wholesale price index in Great Britain for the 1939-46 period.

Source: Through 1976, from *The Golden Constant* by Roy W. Jastram. From 1977, our estimates based on procedure described in main source.

Chart 5

PURCHASING POWER OF GOLD AND OF THE U.S. DOLLAR, 1792-1994

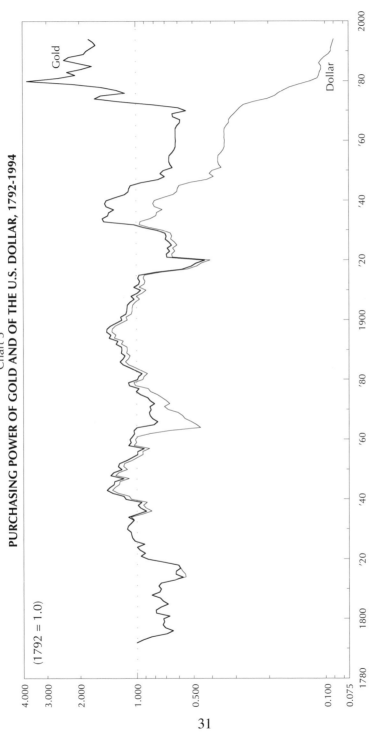

Note: On April 2, 1792, Congress established the dollar (then legally equivalent to 24.75 grains of pure gold) as the Nation's monetary unit. The changes in purchasing power shown in the chart were calculated from annual averages of the wholesale price index (source: U.S. Department of Labor) and the annual averages of the exchange ratio of dollars for gold.

31

The Economics of Gold Mining

As mentioned above, the gold mining industry plays a key role in regulating the annual increments to the gold supply. Gold mining has contributed importantly to the success of gold as money and to the gold standard as a monetary system. Despite this long record of success, critics of the gold standard assert that such a system is left to the mercy and whims of a single industry, driven by its own desire for profit and not by the monetary requirements of a wider economy. There are four main reasons for rejecting such claims. They all relate to the fact that gold mining is subject to the laws of economics.

First, the relevant supply of base money under a gold standard system is all the gold that has ever been mined and accumulated throughout history, not merely its annual increment. Consequently, even if today's gold mining companies were arbitrary about their production policies (a dubious assumption), they can influence only a small fraction of the total gold money supply. This applies equally to gold mining in countries, such as Russia and South Africa, that suffer political or labor instability.

Second, under a gold standard, with its corollary of free banking, private banks supply paper money convertible into a fixed weight of gold. Since free banks operate on a fractional reserve basis, there is no strict or necessary correspondence between gold supplies and paper money supplies. The supply of privately issued convertible paper money expands and fluctuates in accordance with the needs of trade, which at any time may exceed or fall short of the rate of growth in the gold supply. So the gold mining industry is an important, but by no means a monopoly, supplier of gold or gold-based money.

Third, central to gold's role as a standard of monetary value is the integrity of the unit of account (for example, the dollar) and of its issuers, not merely the supply of such units. In this sense, the status of the gold money supply — and hence the status of its suppliers, the gold mining companies — is relatively unimportant. What is very important is that the definition of the unit of account be fixed and maintained. Of course, it does matter that gold mining companies and private gold mints deliver a sound and reliable product. Historically, both have done so.

Finally, the profit motive of mining companies ensures a smoothly increasing gold money supply. Gold mining companies do not try to influence the aggregate supply of money or the wider economy. They seek profits. There is an incentive to mine as much gold as customers demand, in a cost-effective way. Under a gold standard, profit-seeking gold mining companies always receive the same "price," in dollars, for each ounce of output. This is so because the unit of account is defined as a fixed weight of gold. As such, the "price" of gold in terms of any unit, say the dollar, is also fixed. (We may speak of the "price" of a dollar even though it is not truly a price at all, any more than the price of a yardstick is three feet.) Thus revenue growth for a gold mining company under the gold standard reflects higher output, not higher gold prices. Profits are earned by raising output and lowering costs. The most productive and efficient mining companies survive and prosper. The least costly mines are worked before costlier ones. These outcomes are important to the ongoing success of gold as money. Although gold is a nonrenewable resource, under a gold standard there are profitable inducements to expanding production and exploration.

Why is it that for centuries the annual increment to the aboveground stock of gold has been no more than a small fraction of that stock? The factors determining profits in gold mining provide the answer. When economic activity and trade — and hence the demand for gold or gold-based money — grows faster than the prevailing rate of change in the gold stock, prices generally fall. For gold mining companies, this means costs (labor, materials, etc.) also fall. The result is that gold mining profits rise, since the price of gold (revenue) remains unchanged. Higher profits are an inducement to produce more gold, which counteracts falling prices. Conversely, when economic activity slows, so does the demand for gold and gold-based money relative to the prevailing rate of change in gold supplies. Prices generally rise. Gold mining profit margins narrow. Gold output is lowered, counteracting the general rise in prices. In both cases, growth in the supply of gold either is hastened or slowed, not as a result of gold mining companies considering aggregate factors, but in response to changes in their profit margins. Yet the aggregate effect of such profit-seeking is to keep the annual growth of the gold supply, as well as the annual rate of change among prices generally, within a relatively narrow range.

Prices, Cycles, and Growth Under the Gold Standard

Competition among gold mining companies and private banks under a gold standard system with free banking tends to keep the purchasing power of money stable over long periods of time. As such, prices in general tend to be stable, since prices reflect the value of money. Prices rise when the purchasing power of money falls and fall when the purchasing power of money rises. Of course, prices of particular goods still rise and fall to reflect specific supply and demand pressures. But under a gold standard there is no sustained rise or fall in prices generally. A gold standard neither suffers from inflating nor deflating. Gold can neither be printed nor destroyed. While there always is some risk of inflating or deflating under fractional reserve banking, the commitment to making paper money convertible into gold ensures that such risks are minimized, and self-correcting.

International economic integration is fostered under a gold standard with free banking. Gold is accepted as money all over the world. Paper money obligations to pay gold are made by private banks, not national governments. Although by historical evolution there exist specific units of account unique to different peoples of the world (the dollar, the pound, the franc), such units are linked together under a gold standard. Each is defined as a specific weight in gold. Moreover, under free banking currencies denominated in these units of account are the obligations of private banks whose business theoretically knows no borders. The importing and exporting of gold is left free. There are no government efforts undertaken to shield national economies from economic influences abroad or impose protectionist barriers. A gold standard with fixed international exchange rates permits a genuine internationalization of trade and investment. Producers can specialize in goods in which they have a comparative advantage and savers can search beyond national borders for profitable investment opportunities, without the risk of capital loss due to exchange rate fluctuations.

Markets are global and prices are set on world markets under a gold standard. The process David Hume (1752) first described as the "price-specie flow mechanism" ensures that prices are stabilized and gold is evenly distributed in the world to support economic activity. How does this mechanism operate? Suppose prices generally are falling in one country relative to others. That country's exports will rise faster than its imports. Gold will flow in to pay for those exports, stabilizing prices. Conversely, if prices generally are rising in one country relative to others, that country's imports will outpace its exports. Gold will flow out to pay for those exports, once again stabilizing prices. Gold contributes to the integration of global prices and production. Gold is world money.

There also are "income effects" that bring equilibrium under a gold standard. All else equal, countries experiencing relatively faster economic growth exhibit a rising demand for money and falling prices. Gold flows toward such countries, where its value is relatively higher, away from slower growing countries, where its value is lower. Prices stop falling and stabilize in the faster-growing country. Thus international equilibrium is achieved. Capital flows are also integral to the working of the gold standard. Suppose there is an increase in the stock of gold in one country relative to another, after which there develops an excess demand for financial securities in the home country. A greater demand for securities leads to lower interest rates in the home country relative to other countries. Gold flows abroad in search of higher returns. The initial rise in the gold stock in the home country is reversed, again bringing world interest rates and gold holdings into equilibrium.

Under a gold standard, one would expect to find long-run price level stability, although it may take some period for generally rising or declining prices to be reversed. The expectation that prices will revert to an intermediate level fosters stability and long-range business planning. Long-run price level stability is a key characteristic of a gold standard. Changes in the demand for money — what economists call "velocity" — are accommodated by changes in the supply, consisting of gold coin, bank currency, and checking deposits. According to Harvard economist Robert Barro:

> Although changes in the ratio of "money" to its commodity backing or shifts in velocity can influence the price level, the system possesses an important nominal anchor in the fixed price of the reserve commodity. By way of contrast ... under a fiat (government-issue) currency system ... there is no obvious nominal anchor that prescribes some likely limits to changes in the absolute price level.... An important aspect of the gold standard or similar standards in relation to a fiat system is the (partial) separation of price level determination from government policy.... In relation to a fiat currency regime, the key element of the commodity standard is its potential automaticity and consequent absence of political control over the quantity of money and absolute price level.... The gold standard actually prevailed for a substantial period, whereas the world has yet to see a fiat currency system that has obvious "stability" properties. (Barro, 1979.)

The gold standard does not deliver stability of prices by restricting the growth in the money supply to some predetermined rate, as monetarists would have central banks do to maintain price stability under fiat money. Fluctuations in the money supply under a gold standard reflect the market's demand for money, which in turn reflects the need to circulate production and trade. There can be large increases (or decreases) in the money supply under a gold standard, reflecting rapid expansions in economic growth, without a rise (or fall) in the purchasing power of money. Since the money supply under the gold standard is not simply gold coin but also bank currency and checking deposits (with fractional reserve backing), variations in money demand can be accommodated. In the process, the monetary standard remains intact and the price level remains anchored. In the same way, a free market may produce more (or fewer) yardsticks to support greater (or lesser) building construction, without sacrificing the integrity of yardsticks. Indeed, only by maintaining the integrity of money can markets deliver sound money and sustainable economic growth. Under a gold standard, the quality of money matters more than its quantity. Greater supplies of high-quality money pose no special difficulty.

A gold standard operates most efficiently under free banking. It cannot be centrally planned, as under central banking. This is why central banking and the gold standard have not coincided for very long. (See Chapter VII,

"Central Banking and Gold.") As economist Larry Sechrest has observed:

> There are two serious shortcomings of a centrally managed gold standard. First, to work efficiently, such a system requires that a (temporarily) inflationary country must lose specie because of the concomitant trade deficit. A (temporarily) deflationary country must gain specie because of its trade surplus. This makes for a system that is (1) integrated internationally and (2) self-correcting. However, central banks may thwart this process by indulging in "sterilization." That is, central banks are able in the short run to offset the effects of international gold flows on their domestic money stocks. This they undertake in an attempt to insulate the domestic economy from actions abroad. Sterilization reduces the equilibrating virtues of the gold standard.
>
> Second, from a purely domestic standpoint, central banks — even on a gold coin standard — may not respond appropriately to a change in the demand for money. If the fraction of income consumers wish to hold as money changes, then the money supply should change in the same direction. This occurs under free banking because free banks have clear market signals to guide their actions. The signals conveyed by the processes of reflux and adverse clearings lead free banks to monetary equilibrium. Assuming that central banks are nonprofit, "public interest" agencies, consumer demands for redemption (reflux) may not constrain central bank actions. This is obviously true when central banks decide to suspend payments (refuse to honor redemption demands), and suspension was not unknown among central banks on a gold standard. Furthermore, central banks experience no adverse clearings. That is, they do not have to settle accounts with other banks vis-à-vis either notes or checks (at least not domestically). As a result, short-run monetary imbalances become likely. (Sechrest, 1993, pp. 67-68.)

A gold standard operated by a free banking system does not attempt to "insulate" any country from economic influences elsewhere. Rather, it recognizes the advantages of international economic specialization and integration. It is no part of a mercantilist policy of maximizing one's domestic advantage at the expense of neighbors. Just as there is no benefit, for example, in "insulating" New York from the economic developments in California, there is no benefit in insulating the United States from economic developments in Japan — or anywhere else. All benefits are on the side of economic integration, on the widest possible division of labor, and on each nation having full access to the resources and talents of others.

A free banking system also takes advantage of dispersed knowledge. It is able to calibrate its money creation and loan supply to the specific demands of customers. Guided by the profit motive, there is an incentive to minimize mistakes in this regard. Cumulatively, of course, there is an equality between money demand and money supply and between credit demand and credit supply. Central banks, on the other hand, have neither the information nor the incentive to bring the supply of money or credit in line with the needs of markets, especially when not on a gold standard, but even on a gold standard. Central banks have no direct contact with bank customers. Nor are central banks motivated by profit. If their policies are right they do not directly benefit. If their policies are wrong they do not suffer. This detachment from profit-seeking does not make central bank policies more "poised" than those of free banks. On the contrary, central bank policy alternates between excessive and deficient supplies of money and credit, a major source of economic inefficiency and of boom-bust business cycles.

Business-cycle fluctuations are relatively mild under a gold standard operated by free banks, not only because there is equilibrium between the supply and demand of money and credit, but also because interest rates are relatively stable. Interest rates reflect real returns on capital. Investment flows away from sectors with lower returns toward sectors with higher returns. Thus interest rates, like all market prices, provide signals. Interest rates are also a cost of doing business. All else equal, higher interest rates lower profits and lower interest rates raise profits. Thus interest rates both reflect and determine the rate of profit, and hence the output of an economy.

Interest rates also reflect the purchasing power of money. When the value of money is declining or is expected to continue doing so, interest rates rise. An "inflation premium" is factored into nominal interest rates as lenders seek to recapture or anticipate lost purchasing power. Under money of fluctuating value, in contrast, there are periodic redistributions of wealth from creditors to debtors (under unanticipated price inflation) and from debtors to creditors (under unanticipated price deflation). But since the purchasing power of money under a gold standard is relatively stable, interest rates are low and stable as well. Long-term stability in the value of money promotes "deep" capital markets — those with many participants, and therefore efficiency and low-cost capital. There is no inflation premium or deflation discount. Relationships between debtors and creditors are stable because the value of money is stable. Credit arrangements can be undertaken over longer-term maturities. Business calculation and planning can take place with a reliable monetary yardstick. Malinvestments and misallocations of resources, hence business cycles, are minimized.

There are a number of preconditions for healthy and sustainable economic growth. Property rights, the rule of law, low tax rates, and free trade are among them. Sound money is just as important for growth. Stable prices and interest rates provide the best climate for business planning and production, and that is what a gold standard delivers. There is no truth to the claim that a gold standard makes an economy prone to deflation and depression, or that economic growth is held back by deficient supplies of

37

"hard money," or that prosperity and job growth are enhanced by the "stimulative" effects of inflating. A gold standard operates with no bias toward deflating or inflating. Gold can neither be printed nor destroyed. Gold provides a solid and reliable foundation for economic growth.

Public Finance Under the Gold Standard

How do governments finance their operations under a gold standard? First, it should be recognized that the gold standard requires particular principles of conduct and a legal context, namely a respect for property rights, the rule of law, and a strictly limited government (see Chapter V, "Political and Legal Issues"). The operations of government are ideally limited to such areas as police, courts, and national defense — the protection of individual rights, as envisioned by America's Founding Fathers. For the most part such operations are paid for by taxation or fees. Government can insist that taxes be paid in the market's medium of exchange — gold or gold-based money. Government checking accounts are maintained at private banks, but without favoritism to particular institutions.

Nothing inherent in a gold standard system precludes government from borrowing funds to bridge timing differences between the receipt of tax revenues and expenditures. Such timing differences would be most acute in times of war. However, under a gold standard, a government still can borrow by issuing bonds in the open market, subject to investors' assessment of a government's overall credit quality. A government's borrowing capacity will depend ultimately on the ability and willingness of producers under that government to pay taxes. What a gold standard does preclude is chronic deficit spending by government to finance operations that are not otherwise supported by taxation.

Second, it should be emphasized that under a genuine gold standard there is no central banking and no legal tender laws. Hence there is no privileged vehicle by which government can issue bonds not otherwise accepted in the market, nor by which it can gain monopoly access to the creation of inconvertible paper money. Government cannot "monetize" its deficits; it cannot print money, as it does today (see Chapter VII, "Central Banking and Gold"). There is no "seignorage," the process by which government gains revenue from its monopoly on money and its policy of perpetual inflation. Gold money is incompatible with chronic deficit spending. It is not coincidental that the last balanced budget by the U.S. Government occurred in 1969 — 2 years before the abandonment of the international gold standard (see Chart 6). Those who seek to balance the budget by Constitutional amendment seem unaware of the fact that it was the previous abandonment of an existing Constitutional requirement of gold money (Article I, Section 8) that made deficits possible.

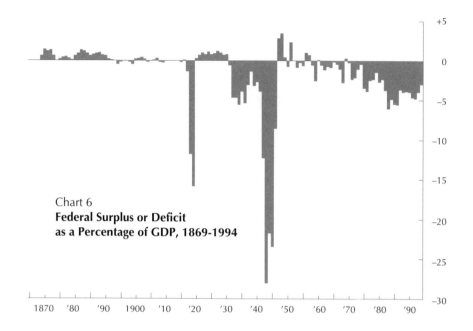

Chart 6
**Federal Surplus or Deficit
as a Percentage of GDP, 1869-1994**

IV.

THE CLASSICAL GOLD STANDARD

THE "classical gold standard" was the predominantly free-market monetary system that operated in the industrializing world for more than a century before World War I. The system was not free of government manipulation or intervention, but it was freer than any other monetary system in history. The classical gold standard did not come apart by its own internal failure, as many assert. It was massive government intervention during World War I that brought an abrupt end to this widely respected system (see Chapter VI, "Subversion of the Gold Standard"). While it lasted, the classical gold standard accompanied a century of unprecedented human freedom, economic prosperity, and peace.

When economists refer to the pre-World War I gold standard as "classical," it is not by accident, but by virtue of hindsight. The system proved superior to all subsequent gold-based regimes, primarily because it was the one left most free to operate. Thus the classical gold standard is the standard against which all other gold-based systems are measured. It is the "gold standard" of gold standards.

A Gold Coin Standard

Under the classical gold standard, gold coin circulated as a medium of exchange alongside privately issued, gold-convertible bank currency and checks. Although some gold was held in bullion form for purposes of savings, gold coin played an active role in everyday monetary circulation.* There were virtually no legal restrictions on a citizen's right to exchange gold coin for currency, or currency for gold coin, at a fixed rate, anywhere in the world. Of course, by tradition every country had its own unit of account, such as the pound in England, the dollar in the United States, and the franc in France. Since these and other currencies throughout the world were defined as specific weights of gold, they were all interchangeable at a fixed rate. Money under the classical gold standard was truly global. The world effectively used one kind of money, and that money was gold.

---

* The use of gold coin in hand-to-hand circulation was greater where banking was less developed or less trusted, as in the Western states (and a double eagle made a very satisfying sound when tossed on the bar after a long cattle drive). Where banking was more developed, the use of gold coin was commonplace only for somewhat ceremonial payments (such as holiday gifts, compensation of directors after a board meeting, etc.). This did not mean that gold was not used or not vital to the monetary system. It was the only legal tender in all circumstances and it was used to settle accounts between banks and countries. Bank notes and checks were readily accepted in payment only because they could be converted into gold on demand, but paper money was not legal tender. In fact, the phrase "legal tender" was not commonly used until governments forced people to accept paper instead of coin.

41

Britain was on the gold standard for nearly 2 centuries, from 1717 to 1914, with the exception of the period 1797-1821, when it suspended convertibility during the Napoleonic Wars. The United States was effectively on a silver standard until 1834 (see Appendix A), thereafter, it was on the gold standard until 1914, with the exception of the Greenback era (1862-1879). No other countries have been on a gold standard for so long and, not coincidentally, no others have ever been so relatively prosperous as these two were during their gold standard eras. Contrary to popular belief today, gold money is not inherently deflationary and not an impediment to economic growth and prosperity. General price levels were flat or actually declining in Britain and the United States during periods of rapid growth, an outcome that many economists today consider an impossible contradiction.

Many countries used both silver and gold interchangeably in the 18th and 19th centuries. By 1880, all industrial countries had converged on gold for economic reasons. More prosperous countries found the higher value of gold more suitable to the circulation of output than silver, while poorer ones tended to use silver. Government attempts to fix a ratio between the two metals to encourage the use of both — a policy known as bimetallism — generally failed. Some governments tried to push silver on an unwilling public, usually driven by the mistaken notion that there was "not enough gold." Such populist experiments proved costly. In 1890 in the United States, for example, Congress passed the Sherman Silver Purchase Act, which provided for limited monetization of silver in order to inflate prices and help debt-ridden farmers. But the Act stoked fears that the United States might abandon the gold standard. There followed a run on the U.S. Treasury's stock of gold, a banking panic in 1893, and a near-depression. In 1896, the silver interests were defeated in the national election.

That the classical gold standard rested on the circulation of gold coin provided an important discipline on currency issuers. Depositors could more easily convert their currency for coin than they could for bullion. One of the first subversions of this system in World War I involved governments removing gold coin from private hands and melting it into more cumbersome gold bullion to impede convertibility.

How the Classical Gold Standard Worked

The classical gold standard was an "automatic" monetary system that did not require government "assistance" or intervention in order to succeed. There were incentives for private banks, gold mining companies, and depositors to operate the system in an efficient manner. Nor was its operation dominated by a handful of large private banks. The classical gold standard was simultaneously decentralized and integrated. It was decentralized because it involved numerous issuers of gold-based money (pri-

42

vate banks). Thus, mistakes by single banks did not reverberate through the entire monetary system, as occurs under central banking. But the classical gold standard was also integrated because it involved the issuance of currency convertible into a single form of money (gold), denominated in units of account defined as weights of gold. From 1821 to 1914, England maintained the pound at a fixed weight of gold, as the United States did for the dollar from 1834 to 1933 (with the exception of the Greenback era from 1862 to 1879). During this period an ounce of gold was worth $20.67; in turn, the British pound was worth $4.86. Other countries at the time also defined their currencies in terms of gold and were convertible. This made for a truly international monetary system.

Before World War I and the dissolution of the classical gold standard, 59 countries participated in the system. Throughout Europe and North America (except Mexico), most of Asia (except China), and most of South America currencies were convertible into gold. Changes in the general level of prices in one country were offset by an automatic balance-of-payments adjustment described in Chapter III as the "price specie-flow" mechanism. For example, if the general level of prices in the United States fell, its exports became relatively more attractive to foreigners, exports then grew relative to imports, there followed an influx of gold to pay for them, and this influx contributed to reversing the initial fall in prices. When the general level of prices in the United States rose, the opposite occurred, leading ultimately to an outflow of gold from the United States and a reversal of the initial rise in prices. This automatic mechanism served to keep prices in line across the world and relatively stable over time.

Not only were prices relatively stable during the classical gold standard, but exchange rates held fast. This permitted capital to flow freely across borders (McKinnon, 1988). The 19th century was an era of relatively free emigration. The gold standard helped make both developments possible. Governments refrained from manipulating (devaluing) their currencies for temporary trade advantage, recognizing it would only invite retaliation. The credibility of world currencies permitted the bulk of international trade to be conducted on credit, thereby economizing on the transport of gold. Immigration was seen as less of a threat when it accompanied prosperity.

Gold production under the classical gold standard adhered closely to the principles of gold mining outlined in Chapter III. The interaction between the real value of gold (its purchasing power) and its mint price (as reflected in units of account such as the dollar) ensured that sufficient quantities of gold were produced to meet demand. A rise in the value of gold meant a greater demand for gold, a fall in other prices generally, a widening of gold mining profit margins, and an inducement to produce more gold. A fall in the value of gold meant a smaller demand for gold, a rise in other prices generally, a narrowing of gold mining profit margins, and a lower rate of gold production. Gold production was efficiently distributed and it adjusted to meet market demand.

Growth in the world's annual output of gold (as a portion of the aboveground stock) fluctuated between $1/4$ and 4 percent during the 19th century (see Chart 3). There was no "shortage" of gold under the classical gold standard, despite the unprecedented rise in economic activity, banking, and trade. Between 1821 and 1914, the world's total stock of gold rose from 123 million fine ounces to 760 million. Large gold discoveries in California and Australia in the middle of the 19th century and in South Africa at the end of the century were spurred in large part by increases in the value of gold. The supply of private bank currency and checking accounts convertible into gold also increased alongside gold coin. But the vast expansion in money supplies under the classical gold standard occurred in response to a rising market demand. This increase in the quantity of money did not cause a decline in its purchasing power because the *quality* of money was maintained. Inflating arose whenever governments suspended the gold standard, issued inconvertible paper money, or devalued.

That the workings of the classical gold standard were automatic is not to say the system lacked intricacy or sophistication. Indeed, it was a highly complex mechanism, so much so that few economists fully understood its unique workings until after it was undermined during World War I. The system evolved from the interaction of banks, businesses, and depositors, none of whom designed it, but each of whom benefited from it in their own way. From another perspective, the workings of the classical gold standard were simple and elegant. Surely the system suffered from little of the complexity that has overwhelmed today's central bankers who try vainly to manage fiat paper money.

Economists in the 19th century tended to take for granted the smooth functioning of the gold standard or to assume central banks like the Bank of England made it possible. Most modern critics of the gold standard are critical of the gold exchange standard that operated after World War I. Nevertheless, even these critics have applauded the success of the much freer classical gold standard in the 19th century. Eichengreen, for example, who interprets the gold standard as a "fetter" upon the freedom of economies to grow, has written the following:

> There can be no question that the development of the international gold standard in the second half of the 19th century and the enormous growth of international trade and investment which took place are no mere coincidences. The hallmark of the prewar gold standard was precisely its ability to accommodate disturbances to financial markets without causing severe business cycle fluctuations.... For more than a quarter of a century before WWI,

44

the gold standard provided the framework for domestic and international monetary relations. Currencies were convertible into gold on demand and linked internationally at fixed exchange rates. Gold shipments were the ultimate means of balance of payments settlement. The gold standard had been a remarkably efficient mechanism for organizing financial affairs. No global crisis comparable to the one that began in 1929 had disrupted the operation of the financial markets. No economic slump comparable to that of the 1930s had so depressed output and employment. (Eichengreen, 1992.)

Free Banking versus Central Banking

The classical gold standard enjoyed its greatest success when it was operated by private banks guided by the profit motive. The 19th century was characterized by systems of relatively free banking. Banking systems were largely devoid of monopoly powers on the issuance of money and of subsidies such as government deposit insurance. Contrary to popular accounts, free banking was neither chaotic nor harmful to money integrity and economic growth. On the contrary, free banking was integral to the success of the classical gold standard. When legal restrictions were imposed on private banking, inefficiency and instability due to occasional suspensions of convertibility did occur. Gold was not to blame.

Central banks were either nonexistent or relatively passive participants in the 19th century monetary mechanism. There was no central bank to speak of in the United States from 1836 to 1913. Private banks, operating under relatively few restrictions and without Federal deposit insurance coverage, issued gold-convertible currency as part of the international gold standard. Canada had no central bank until 1935. The Bank of England had been established in Great Britain as early as 1694, but private banks still issued gold-convertible currency in the 19th century. With some exceptions, the Bank of England followed what became known as the "rules of the game" under the gold standard. Briefly, these rules ensured that bank lending would be restrained and interest rates would increase* when gold reserves decreased and *vice versa.*

The growth of central banking generally came to undermine the workings of the classical gold standard, because the central banks' allegiance to sponsoring governments grew, and they increasingly broke the rules. Such breaches accelerated during World War I (see Chapter VI).

A Century of Sound Money

The classical gold standard was not perfectly free of government intervention, but it was the freest monetary system ever achieved. The extent of

---

* Not very much by today's standards, however. A governor of the Bank of England once remarked that an interest rate of 6 percent "would bring gold right out of the ground."

its freedom suggests why there existed a century of sound money in the world. Gold production and convertible private bank currency both expanded rapidly in the 19th century in response to growing demand. Yet price levels in 1914 were not much different from those in 1821. According to Bordo (1980, p. 8), the long-term trend over this period was one of gently falling prices. Prices fell at a rate of only 0.4 percent per year in Britain (1821-1914) and only 0.1 percent per year in the United States (1834-1913). Falling prices accompanied relatively low rates of unemployment and high rates of economic growth. The Keynesian economists who still dominate today's profession and believe inflation "oils the wheels of commerce" regard noninflationary growth as impossible. Why did the classical gold standard work? Michael Bordo observes that:

> One important implication of the tendency for price levels to revert toward a long-run stable value under the gold standard was that it insured a measure of predictability with respect to the value of money: though prices would rise or fall for a few years, inflation or deflation would not persist. Such belief in long-run price stability would encourage economic agents to engage in contracts with the expectation that, should prices of commodities or factors of production change, the change would reflect real forces rather than changes in the value of money. (Bordo, 1980, pp. 11-12.)

Greater predictability in business calculation and planning made for greater economic growth. Thus, it was common under the classical gold standard to find railroad bonds with maturities of as long as 100 years. Such a phenomenon disappeared along with the classical gold standard. Long-term capital markets developed in the 19th century because money was trusted and gold was money. Stable price were a reflection of that trust. The world's monetary units of account (the pound, the dollar, etc.) had a fixed definition in terms of gold. Money was truly an invariant yardstick.

There were exceptions to the general stability of money and prices during the 19th century. They generally involved government interventions. The debilitating effects of U.S. Government attempts to expand the use of unwanted silver money for the sake of special interests after the Civil War has already been mentioned. The sacrifice of public finance standards during war time also posed problems. The United States suspended the gold standard during the Civil War, imposed legal tender laws in 1862 to compel the use of Government money (the inconvertible "Greenbacks"), and nationalized private bank notes by requiring that they be collateralized by Government securities. This last measure was designed to ensure a ready market for burgeoning Government deficits.

Gold retained its value throughout this period, but the monetary measures imposed during the Civil War undermined the integrity of substitutes for gold.* "Greenback" inflation was rampant from 1862 until about 1865, at which time legislation was enacted to prepare for a resumption of gold convertibility by 1879. Once resumption took place, price stability returned. Money was again anchored to an objective value. Sound money made for sound banking. Under the classical gold standard, banks were far more conservative than in recent decades. Yet commercial banks still financed new industries. There was no Government deposit insurance to bailout bad banking at the expense of good. The few money panics and currency shortages that did arise were due entirely to regulations forcing banks to purchase Government bonds (Salsman, 1990).

Aside from such war time exceptions, public finance practices under the classical gold standard generally were conservative. Governments balanced their budgets. They borrowed occasionally, but there was no secular rise in public debt levels relative to economic growth, no monetization of government debt by central banks, and no burdensome interest expenses. Government functions and spending levels were fairly restricted. Welfare spending began to rise somewhat in Britain during the middle 19th century and in Germany with the rise of Bismarck in the 1880s, but not much at all in the United States until the 1930s, well after the classical gold standard era. For most of the 19th century, public finance practices were conservative and therefore did not undermine the classical gold standard.

Economic Effects of the Classical Gold Standard

The economic benefits of worldwide monetary integration under the classical gold standard proved significant for those who participated in it. The 19th century witnessed the growth of the industrial revolution beyond Britain into the United States. Whole new industries were created. Real wages rose together with employment opportunities. Living standards skyrocketed. As Michael Bordo has explained,

> The period from 1880 to 1914, known as the heyday of the gold standard, was a remarkable period in world economic history. It was characterized by rapid economic growth, the free flow of labor and capital across political borders, virtually free trade and, in general, world peace.... In several respects, the economic performance in the United States and the United Kingdom was superior under the classical gold standard to that of the subsequent period of managed fiduciary media. In particular, both the price level and real economic activity were more stable in the pre-World War I gold standard period than in the subsequent six-and-one-half decades. (Bordo, 1981.)

Despite the fact of very high rates of economic growth in the 19th century, it was not an age of boom and bust business cycles. According to one

---

* While convertibility was suspended, the New York Stock Exchange maintained a "gold room," where gold was traded to effect international payments.

economic historian, the U.S. experienced no recessions between the end of the Civil War and the onset of World War I (Zarnowitz, 1992, p. 231). What was interpreted at the time as periodic declines in real output are now generally agreed to have involved only declines in *the rate of growth* of output. In other words, a deceleration in annual growth from, say, 8 percent one year to 3 percent the next was felt at the time as a decline in output (a recession). In fact, there was only a temporary slowing down of an otherwise high growth rate. Today, in contrast, economic growth rates of 3 percent are considered quite high and recessions occur every few years.

The periodic episodes of declining prices under the classical gold standard were not an impediment to economic growth, as historical data show. All else equal, falling prices would normally mean falling revenues. But costs, which are prices, also were falling. Thus profit margins were maintained, and indeed widened whenever new business opportunities were uncovered. The spur of profits brought a vast expansion of unit output and revenues. Profits and output could both grow even amidst declining prices. Meanwhile, living standards and real incomes grew significantly. With the rise of industrialism and the greater use of machinery, worker productivity, and hence wages, also grew quickly. This growth in money wages, combined with falling consumer prices, meant a huge increase in real wages. Each dollar of wage thus could buy more goods with every passing year.

Problems of persistent unemployment so characteristic of today's more regulated economies also were less apparent in the more laissez-faire 19th century. In part this reflected relatively freer labor markets compared to today. Instead of government-sponsored unemployment schemes, voluntary private charity was used to support genuine hardship cases. There were no labor unions with government boards forcing employers to deal with them. There were no payroll or income taxes. Bordo calculates unemployment rates in Britain and the United States that were several percentage points lower a century ago than today (1981, p. 13). This performance is particularly remarkable given the rapid rate of increase in the labor force of each country, due not only to higher birth rates and increasing life spans, but immigration from less prosperous regions of the world. Growing economies absorbed a growing labor force. With minimal government intervention in labor markets, the standard of living and the working conditions of labor improved enormously throughout the 19th century.

International Economic Integration

As an international monetary system, the classical gold standard helped coordinate the international division of labor. Individuals and countries had the incentive to produce and trade according to their comparative advantage. Not only capital but labor flowed freely across most borders.

Free trade was the rule, not the exception. Beggar-thy-neighbor policies were rare, an important achievement considering that protectionist policies of Mercantilists had reigned in the 18th century. Significantly, international peace reigned for a full century, from the end of the Napoleonic Wars (1815) to World War I (1914). It is not coincidental that this also was the reigning era of the classical gold standard.

The lesson to be learned from the economic success of the 19th century was not that sound money alone was a panacea. Sound money had its beneficial effects, but it was the by-product of the prevailing political philosophy of the 19th century. Classical liberalism was the prevailing political philosophy. Government was strictly limited, especially in the United States after the Constitution of 1789. There was general respect for private property and the rule of law. When this fabric began to be torn during World War I, it also tore away the foundations of the gold standard and sound money.

One symbol of this drastic change was the chain of events that took place in the United States in 1913. The Pujo Committee was blaming banking instabilities on the country's leading bankers instead of on the regulation that caused it. When banker J. P. Morgan testified before the committee, he was asked about the role of gold in the financial system and whether it might be the source of problems. Morgan answered succinctly, "gold is money, and nothing else." Later that year, Congress established the Federal Reserve System to replace the "money monopoly" on Wall Street with a "public-spirited" central bank. In 1917 a law was passed requiring the transfer of gold from banks to the Fed. By 1933, the U.S. Government would default on the gold standard and confiscate private gold.

Respect for the classical gold standard grew in the minds of some perceptive economists during the 1930s. It was a time when the gold-exchange standard that had been managed by central banks broke down and was abandoned amidst a worldwide depression. Money broke loose from its traditional gold moorings and economists were at a loss about what course to chart. Some had a glimpse of what had been achieved in the past. One economist looked back at the classical gold standard "as a perfect mechanism" (Walker, 1933). Another remarked about how "the world that disappeared in 1914 appeared, in retrospect, something like our picture of paradise" (Jones, 1933). The Macmillan Committee in Britain, formed in 1931 to assess the breakdown of money, spoke of "the nineteenth century philosophy of the gold standard," and how it seemed forever lost to the modern world (cited in Walker, 1933). And yet Walker himself maintained at the time that "the precise content of the 'philosophy' is, in fact, however, somewhat difficult to discover, and more so to interpret" (1933).

49

Walker's self-admitted inability to recognize the political underpinnings of gold money was quite common after World War I. Perhaps it explains the absence of any strong intellectual guardians of the classical gold standard in the 1930s, just when gold was being forcibly removed from all the monies of the world. A particular intellectual, political, and legal philosophy stood behind the classical gold standard. When that philosophy declined, so did the gold standard that depended on it. Eventually, the gold standard was completely subverted.

V.

POLITICAL AND LEGAL ISSUES

T HE intellectual and legal climate of the 17th, 18th and 19th centuries generally was favorable to the evolution and operation of the classical gold standard. The rights of individuals increasingly were respected and the pursuit of one's own happiness was considered a legitimate and proper aim. In the Glorious Revolution of 1688, the British monarch was substantially restrained by Parliament for the first time. In America, the Declaration of Independence (1776) spelled out the evils of tyranny and defended the rights of free men while the U.S. Constitution (1787) secured both civil rights and property rights. The intellectual tide supporting this "classical liberalism" was so great that by the mid-19th century Americans would fight a civil war so that political rights could be extended to blacks. By the 19th century, commerce was freer than any time before or since.

Although gold money had evolved as the money of choice over the centuries, political freedom and private property had never been substantially protected until the Renaissance and Enlightenment. They received such protection under common law in Britain and under constitutionally limited government in the United States. In the 18th and 19th centuries, the rule of law replaced the rule of men. A high value was placed on the credibility of promises and sanctity of contract. The primary function of government, especially as established in the United States, was to uphold private property and voluntary contract. The classical gold standard evolved in this intellectual and legal climate. When governments failed to defend property rights, as happened on occasion during the 19th century and increasingly so in the 20th, freedom, gold money, and the gold standard were all jeopardized.

The Meaning of Gold

A code of conduct is required for men to live successfully and with one another. A division of labor and specialization are indispensable for prosperity, and this is impossible without commerce. Throughout history, to the extent men have been left free to produce and trade, they have been able to survive and prosper. The historical convergence on gold as money was a crucial element of this successful evolution. However, gold money is as crucial to maintaining a prosperous civilization as it is to creating one.

Unfortunately, this has not always been acknowledged by intellectuals, even as it has been indispensable to producers and consumers. The pursuit of material wealth has been condemned as evil, for example, by the religionists who dominated during the poverty-stricken Dark Ages. Such crit-

51

ics persist today, sometimes in religious form, but also in secular varieties. Philosopher-novelist Ayn Rand posed a rhetorical question to such critics:

> So you think that money is the root of all evil? Have you ever asked what is the root of money? Money is a tool of exchange, which can't exist unless there are goods produced and men able to produce them. Money is the material shape of the principle that men who wish to deal with one another must deal by trade and give value for value.... Money is made possible only by the men who produce. When you accept money in payment for your effort, you do so only on the conviction that you will exchange it for the product of the effort of others. It is not the moochers and the looters who give value to money. Not an ocean of tears or all the guns in the world can transform those pieces of paper in your wallet into the bread you will need to survive tomorrow. Those pieces of paper, which should have been gold, are a token of honor — your claim upon the energy of the men who produce. Your wallet is your statement of hope that somewhere in the world around you there are men who will not default on the moral principle which is the root of money.... Money permits no deals except those to mutual benefit by the unforced judgment of the traders.... When men live by trade — with reason, not force as their final arbiter — it is the best product that wins, the best performance, the men of best judgment and highest ability — and the degree of a man's productiveness is the degree of his reward. This is the code of existence whose tool and symbol is money. Is this what you consider evil? (Rand, 1957, p. 410-411.)

This is the meaning of gold money that was held implicitly by thinkers of the Enlightenment and by statesmen who helped form and lead limited governments (perhaps they took it for granted). This is the principle that stands behind what Scherman (1938) calls "the promises men live by." Property is not theft, as Proudhon claimed. Property is created wealth, protected by law. Property arises from the mutual interaction of free and productive individuals. Gold money represents and makes possible produced wealth, the only kind possible to men, and is nothing without that wealth. Gold in this sense is "honest money." The gold standard is not an expediency relevant to some eras but not others. The gold standard is a monetary standard of honesty and integrity. As journalist-economist Henry Hazlitt once observed, "the gold standard is not an isolated gadget, but an integral part of a system of free enterprise and limited government, of good faith and law, of promise-keeping and the sanctity of contract" (Hazlitt, 1975).

Gold and Property Rights

Money, including gold, is property. If it is not protected by law it is jeopardized. Economic activity — the creation of property — cannot flourish under either anarchy or statism. The legal stability and long-range planning required to produce and save wealth are undermined by the initiation of force and by seizures, whether inflicted by marauding gangs or by interventionist governments. The protection of private property is indispensable to economic development. By the 18th century, the common law in Britain had progressed to the point at which it regarded money as private property whose value could not be undermined by government. The economic success of Britain and the United States in the 18th and 19th centuries was due in large part to legal protections of private property. Such protection was neither perfect nor consistent, but to the extent it was provided at all, gold money and material prosperity flourished. The classical gold standard flowed naturally from limitations on government.

Coinage is best left for private industry under a sound gold standard. Government should prevent fraud that might arise in the coin industry, as in others, but cannot become a producer of coins itself without engendering conflicts of interest. The government cannot be both an arbiter of contracts and a party to them. The same principle holds in the field of banking. A system of free banking, which stores gold coin, lends it, and issues claims (currency) against it, likewise requires a legal context respectful of private property. According to economist Lawrence White:

> Individual sovereignty in economic affairs amounts to the freedom of potential buyers and sellers to make their own bargains, unimpeded by third-party impositions or barriers. It amounts, in other words, to free trade. A system of free banking entails free trade in the market for bank notes. No legislative barriers are placed in the way of exchanges of bank notes or demand deposits between potential issuers and money users. Individuals are free to accept or reject the liabilities of particular banks as they see fit. Banks are free to pursue whatever policies they find advantageous in the issuing of liabilities and the holding of asset portfolios, subject only to the general legal prohibition against fraud or breach of contract. (White, 1989, pp. 152-153.)

The fact that free banking evolved historically from a strictly warehouse operation to the lending of claims on gold coin meant that free banking would operate on a fractional reserve basis. Thereafter, bank currency no longer represented a warehouse receipt for the same lot of gold initially deposited by a customer, but rather became a liability of the issuing bank, a legal obligation to deliver gold of like fineness whenever the customer demanded it. In turn, currency became an asset for its holder. As discussed in Chapter II, there were sound economic reasons for banks and customers to arrive at such an arrangement. Banks earned money by lending gold and paying depositors some of the interest. Depositors preferred receiving interest income to paying storage fees for 100 percent-reserve accounts. This evolution in the relationship between banks and customers was sanctioned by the law.

Despite the mutual advantages inherent in free banking, some advocates of gold money, such as Rothbard (1983, p. 92), have argued that fractional-reserve banking is inherently fraudulent. They maintain that *only* physical gold is money and that any banking conducted with less than 100 percent reserves amounts to a Ponzi-scheme, a subtle form of theft, and therefore must be outlawed. They believe only safe-deposit and warehouse banking is legitimate. This position rejects an established market choice in banking. It argues for a government-imposed reserve requirement, whereas government regulation of bank reserve-holding behavior is a contravention of free choice in money and banking.

In fact, no fraud arises in a bank reserve arrangement fully understood by the relevant parties. This is the case with free banking. Convertible bank currency and checks are payable to bearers on demand. They represent legal titles to bank-held gold coin. Just as gold coin is property, so are legal claims to gold. The value of such claims depends on the capacity of issuing banks to redeem them. The promise banks live by is the promise to pay gold on demand, not a promise to hold some particular fraction of their outstanding currency in gold reserves. The practice of holding fractional reserves is not itself a breach of contract. Of course, if any bank's promise to redeem its currency on demand is not met, that constitutes a breach of contract. In such a situation, the law must intervene and compel restitution for the injured party. Reserve-holding decisions must be left to the mutual agreement of banks and their customers, shaped exclusively by the forces of competition. The typical result is a variety of conservative reserve-holding behaviors. Nothing inherent in free banking precludes depositors from warehousing gold and other valuables for a fee.

Regardless of a bank's business reputation, if the legal status of its currency is at all in question, then the quality of its money necessarily is also in question. Government must play the role of enforcer of private contracts. When government fails to serve this vital function, or worse, when it dictates the terms of contracts, monetary efficiency and economic prosperity suffer. Free banking cannot survive amidst anarchy. Some of the worst episodes in money and banking history, involving fraud and inflating, arose when currency redemption was not enforced or when government intervened actively to sanction suspensions. Often this was done to alleviate government debt burdens or obtain funds from the private banking system.

Constitutional Aspects of Gold

The standard money used in the United States today is the Federal Reserve note, or currency. All other forms of money — such as checks and electronic debits — are convertible into this currency. Federal Reserve notes, which initially were convertible into gold, now are convertible into nothing except another Federal Reserve note. There is good evidence to support the view that Federal Reserve notes are unconstitutional (Vieira, 1983). Neither the Federal Government nor the states have any power under the U.S. Constitution to issue paper money of any kind. Nor is there any constitutional authority to vest such monetary power in any agency of Government, such as the Federal Reserve System (Timberlake, 1991). The only monetary power of Government under the Constitution is the power to coin precious metals and regulate their exchange ratios with foreign coins. Thus, in the United States, only gold or silver represent constitutional forms of money. How then has it come to pass that fiat paper money reigns?

America's Founding Fathers recognized the dangers of government money and intervention in money. They were aware of the long history of government abuse of coinage dating back to Greece and Rome. The founders knew that whenever emperors and kings feared their subjects would not stand for higher tax burdens, they would frequently resort to debasing money, by "clipping" the edges of coins or diluting the precious metal alloy of coins, as a hidden form of taxation. In the years leading up to ratification of the U.S. Constitution, Americans suffered from government paper money inflating in 9 of the 13 British colonies. American independence under the Articles of Confederation did not improve this monetary situation. According to Dunne (1960, p. 7), the Continental Congress had the power to issue bills of credit and did so as "the principal means of financing the War.... [Congress] used the authority up to the hilt, denouncing anyone who refused to take its continental dollar 'as enemies of the liberties of the United States,' and requested the States ... to make its paper a legal tender." A popular expression at the time, "not worth a Continental," reflected the contempt held for the paper dollars issued by the Congress. Even though the Articles of Confederation promised that each Continental dollar would be paid in full, they eventually were redeemed for only a tiny fraction of par. Many were not turned in at all, presumably because they had been discarded as worthless.

Thus America's Founding Fathers were well aware of the dangers inherent in government issuing money. Once the Constitutional Convention got underway in the summer of 1787, there was heated debate about government monetary powers. The framers of the U.S. Constitution were heavily influenced by John Locke's defense of private property, by the British common law tradition favoring private money, and by the *Commentaries* of Blackstone, which provided the source of the phrase in the U.S. Constitution delineating Congress' money powers (see Getman, 1980). What is that power? Article I, Section 8 of the U.S. Constitution gives Congress the power "to coin Money, regulate the Value thereof, and of foreign coin ..."

The debates that took place during the Constitutional Convention about the document's provision and thereafter regarding its ratification make it clear that this power was solely the power to strike off gold and silver coins. No power is granted to the Federal Government or to the states to issue paper currency, then referred to as "bills of credit." As regards the benefits of having this power removed from the states under the newly proposed Constitution, James Madison wrote in *The Federalist (#44)* in 1788:

> The extension of the prohibition to bills of credit must give pleasure to every citizen, in proportion to his love of justice and his knowledge of the true springs of public prosperity. The loss which America has sustained since the peace, from the pestilent effects of paper money on the necessary confidence between man and man, on the necessary confidence in the public councils, on the industry and morals of the people, and on the character of republican government, constitutes an enormous debt ... which can be expatiated no otherwise than by a voluntary sacrifice on the altar of justice, of the power which has been the instrument of it.... The same reasons which show the necessity of denying to the States the power of regulating coin, prove with equal force that they ought not to be at liberty to substitute a paper medium in the place of coin.... The power to make anything other than gold and silver a tender in payment of debts, is withdrawn from the States, on the same principle with that of issuing a paper currency. (Madison, 1788.)

The debates surrounding the Constitution also make clear that the U.S. Federal Government has no power to issue paper money. According to Madison, who took extensive notes at the Convention, a preliminary draft of the Constitution would have given Congress the power "To borrow money and emit bills on the credit of the United States." However, Madison reports in August of 1787 that "Mr. Govr. Morris moved to strike out 'and emit bills on the credit of the U. States' — If the United States had credit, such bills would be unnecessary; if they had not, unjust and useless" (1788, Volume II, p. 413). In other words, if the Government's need of funds truly was sound, it could easily borrow. There would be no reason under such conditions for Government to resort to printing paper money. On the other hand, if the Government's credit was unsound, it would be unjust to issue paper money.

Still, some delegates to the Convention objected to the prohibition against Government paper money, arguing that if Congress were not given the express power to issue paper money, it would never again possess such power. Indeed, that was a fair reading of the Constitution, which established a Government of limited and enumerated powers, pursuant to which the Congress had only such powers as were specifically granted. One delegate, Mr. Mercer, opposed the prohibition on government paper money, saying "it would stamp suspicion on the government to deny it a discretion on this point." He believed that it was "impolitic also to excite the opposition of all those who were friends of paper money" and stressed that "the people of property would be sure to be on the side of the plan, and it was impolitic to purchase their further attachment with the loss of the opposite class of Citizens" (Madison, 1788, p. 413). Mercer's appeal to unrestricted state power and class envy was at odds with the framers' general intent to limit the power of government and to minimize the spread of factions that would invite special interests and legislative privileges. Mercer recognized that fiat paper money threatened property rights, but contrary to the views of most delegates, he did not seem to mind it.

Based on experience, the majority of delegates to the Constitutional Convention opposed government money. One proponent, Mr. Ellsworth, reflected the majority view that "this is a favorable moment to shut and bar the door against paper money. The mischiefs of the various experiments which had been made, were now fresh in the public mind and had excited the disgust of all the respectable part of America." Ellsworth was speaking of course, not of private money, but of government money. The motion by Morris to strike the phrase about government paper money passed, 9 to 2. The framers expressly rejected the case for unlimited state discretion and class warfare offered by Mercer.

What did the framers intend by granting Congress the power "to regulate the value" of coinage? Only the power to set the dollar's definition in terms of gold and silver and to determine the metal content of its coinage. The aim was not to have a government money, nor to change its value perpetually, nor to regulate private money and banking. The goal was simply to codify an already widely established monetary *standard*. As discussed in Chapter IV, a monetary standard is like a yardstick, a recognition that a yard is equivalent to three feet. Thus a dollar also was to be defined as a certain weight in precious metals. Not coincidentally, the coinage provisions in Article I, Section 8 are followed closely by the provision allowing Congress to set weights and measures. According to Madison "the regulation of weights and measures … is founded on like considerations with the preceding power of regulating coin" (*The Federalist, #42*). Thus the U.S. Constitution gave Congress the relatively innocuous power of codifying what markets had already arrived at in various weights and measures, including those pertinent to hard money. A pound of sugar, for example, must weigh 16 ounces, and a yard of lumber must contain three feet. This reflects the legitimate power of government to uphold rights and prohibit fraud. The Founding Fathers believed it applied as much to money as it did to other measures. Government violates rights by debasing money just as much as by restricting free speech.

Gold and Liberty

The U.S. Constitution represented a legal watershed in the history of gold money. It recognized that gold *is* money, that money is *property*, and that gold money deserves legal *protection*. Moreover, the U.S. Constitution and its framers clearly implied that government's only proper monetary function is to protect property rights and prohibit fraud in private money, not to create or regulate money directly. This relatively brief episode must be seen as the high point in any history of free market money. This legal framework paved the way for a century of relatively free money and banking. In the United States, the dollar maintained its value for most of the following century-and-a-quarter. The classical gold standard and laissez-faire capitalism prevailed. Economic growth and prosperity in the United States reached levels unseen in all of history. These practical results reflect the fact that gold and political liberty go hand in hand. As economist Joseph Schumpeter has observed:

> An 'automatic' gold currency is part and parcel of a laissez-faire and free-trade economy. It links every nation's money rates and price levels with the money rates and price levels of all other nations that are on gold. It is extremely sensitive to government expenditure and even to attitudes or policies that do not involve expenditure directly, for example, to foreign policy, to certain policies of taxation, and, in general, to precisely all those policies that violate the principles of economic liberalism. *This* is the reason why gold is so unpopular now and also why it was so popular in a bourgeois era. It imposes restrictions upon governments and bureaucracies that are much more powerful than is parliamentary criticism. It is both the badge and the guarantee of bourgeois freedom — of freedom not simply of the bourgeois *interest*, but of freedom in the bourgeois *sense*. From this standpoint a man might quite rationally fight for it, even if fully convinced of the validity of all that has ever been urged against it on economic grounds. From the standpoint of statism and planning, a man may not less rationally condemn it, even if fully convinced of the validity of all that has ever been urged for it on economic grounds. (Schumpeter, 1954, pp. 405-406.)

Schumpeter's observation captures the fact that gold and gold-based money reflect a particular political context favorable to liberty and capitalism. The rise of gold currency is not a case of one class emerging victorious against another but of all men advancing, of freedom victorious against serfdom. This relationship has been recognized by economists from a range of schools, by free bankers and central bankers, by those who defend gold money and those who attack it, by those who defend political freedom and those who do not. Alan Greenspan has argued that "gold and economic freedom are inseparable, that the gold standard is an instrument of laissez-faire and that each implies and requires the other" (Greenspan, 1967). Business economist Benjamin Anderson once noted:

> Those who have an adult's recognition and an adult's understanding of the world which preceded the first World War look back upon it with a great nostalgia. There was a sense of security then which has never since existed. Progress was generally taken for granted.... We had a prolonged period in which decade after decade had seen increasing political freedom, the progressive spread of democratic institutions, the steady lifting of the standard of life for the masses of men.... In financial matters the good faith of governments was taken for granted.... No country took pride in debasing its currency as a clever financial expedient. (Anderson, 1920.)

Economist Leland Yeager has written that "by and large, people in countries that happened to be on the gold standard were freer from government control than in any age before or since — freer to transact business, freer to make investments, to transfer funds, to travel.... The civility and internationality prevalent during the age of the (classical) gold standard have such a charm for us nowadays that it seems almost sacrilege to ask whether these benefits resulted from the gold standard, or instead, coexisted with it by mere coincidence" (Yeager, 1984). John Maynard Keynes, long-time critic of the gold standard who once dismissed gold as a "barbarous relic," nevertheless recognized the world's major achievements in the century before World War I:

> What an extraordinary episode in the economic progress of man that age was that came to an end in August 1914!... [A]ny man of capacity or character at all exceeding the average [could escape from the working class] into the middle and upper classes, for whom life offered, at a low cost and with the least trouble, conveniences, comforts and amenities beyond the compass of the richest and most powerful monarchs of other ages.... But, most important of all, he regarded this state of affairs as normal, certain and permanent, except in the direction of further improvement, and any deviation from it as aberrant, scandalous, and avoidable. The projects and politics of militarism and imperialism, of racial and cultural rivalries, of monopolies, restrictions, and exclusion ... appeared to exercise almost no influence at all in the ordinary course of social and economic life, the internationalization of which was nearly complete in practice. (Keynes, 1920, pp. 10-12.)

Gold-based money was an integral part of this economic success. As shown in Chapter VI, this idyllic world disintegrated in the 20th century, when free banking and the classical gold standard were abandoned over most parts of the world. Even in the 19th century, a series of harmful Government interventions and reinterpretations of the intent of the U.S.

Founding Fathers, chipped away at the legal and economic status of gold. Keynes contributed heavily to attacks on gold after World War I.

The Imposition of Legal Tender Laws

One of the most harmful government interventions in money has been legal tender laws. Such laws compel citizens to use particular forms of money, as against market-chosen money. Courts are instructed to uphold only those contracts denominated in legal tender. For example, regardless of what form of money might be agreed upon between two parties to a loan, a debtor legally satisfies his obligation simply by offering legal tender, even if this causes a loss to the creditor. Sometimes legal tender laws apply to a single form of money, establishing a monopoly. Often they apply to inconvertible paper money that does not otherwise warrant market confidence. Governments have granted legal tender status to their own inconvertible paper money. The conflict of interest in such an arrangement should be obvious, as are the results of forcing markets to use unsound money.

No law granting legal tender status to inconvertible government paper money existed in Europe at the time of the American Constitutional Convention. The United States itself had no such law on the books until 1862. Gold and silver had been granted legal tender status under the Constitution, but it represented no obvious injustice, because gold and silver were market-accepted money in any event. The earliest measures taken by Congress to carry out its limited monetary powers could be interpreted easily as consistent with the Constitution. The Coinage Act of 1792 set the value of the dollar as a fixed weight of gold and silver and established the national mint. Private coin minting still continued alongside the new Government mint, however. A year earlier, in 1791, the new Bank of the United States was capitalized, partly with Government funds, in order to refinance part of the Revolutionary War debt. The bank refrained from issuing money of any kind. Its narrow purpose and limited, 20-year charter were consistent with Congress' constitutional power to borrow money. The prevailing antebellum interpretations of government monetary powers were summed up by Daniel Webster:

> Most unquestionably there is no legal tender, and there can be no legal tender in this country, under the authority of this government or any other, but gold and silver — either the coinage of our own mints or of foreign coins, at rates regulated by Congress. This is a constitutional principle perfectly plain, and of the very highest performance. The States are expressly prohibited from making anything but gold and silver a tender in payment of debts, and, although no such express prohibition is applied to Congress, yet, as Congress has no power granted to it in this respect but to coin money, and to regulate the value of foreign coins, it

clearly has no power to substitute paper, or anything else, for coin as a tender in payment of debts and in discharge of contracts. (Webster, 1834.)

Antebellum commentary from the Supreme Court echoed these insights. Oliver Wendell Holmes stressed that the term "coin" should be taken literally:

The power to 'coin money' means to strike off metallic medals (coin), and to make those medals legal tender (money); the Constitution says expressly that Congress shall have power to make metallic legal tender, how can it be taken to say by implication that Congress shall have the power to make money legal tender? (Cited in Getman, 1980.)

Congress was to *coin* money and to regulate the value *thereof*, which meant to regulate the relative values (fix the ratios) between coined money, between domestic coin, and between domestic and foreign coin. As one Supreme Court justice argued in 1830, "the whole [of the Constitution's monetary provisions] was intended to exclude everything from use, as a circulating medium, except gold and silver . . . that the dollar may represent property and not the shadow of it" (cited in Getman, 1980). And the Chief Justice of the Court in 1850 wrote that "the power of coining money and regulating its value was delegated to the Congress by the Constitution for the very purpose, as assigned by the framers of the instrument, of creating and preserving the uniformity of such a standard of value" (cited in Getman, 1980). Thus for most of the antebellum period in the United States, the framers of the Constitution and leading spokesmen in Congress and on the Supreme Court were in fairly close agreement about the limited monetary powers of Government in the United States

Nearly three-quarters of a century had passed after ratification of the U.S. Constitution in 1789 before Congress passed a law granting legal tender status to Government paper money. The Legal Tender Act of 1862 applied to inconvertible Treasury notes, known more popularly as "Greenbacks" for the crude green ink splashed on the reverse side of the notes. The private minting of coins was made forever illegal in the United States starting in 1864. The clear constitutional mandate for metallic money was being flouted. The occasion was the Civil War and the professed goal of the Act was to help pay for it. The Federal Government's capacity to borrow money to pay for the conflict was deemed insufficient. Sheer expedience drove Congress to pass the Legal Tender Act. But it violated personal freedoms no less so than did other acts of the time, such as military conscription and an income tax. Private money and gold still were permitted, and survived the war to some extent. The Greenbacks were severely inflated during the war, but eventually were redeemed for gold. To its credit, the United States returned to the gold standard in 1879 and remained committed to it until World War I.

A number of injured parties challenged the constitutionality of the Legal Tender Act. Unfortunately, a series of Supreme Court decisions, handed down soon after the Civil War (the "Legal Tender Cases"), for the first time in the history of American constitutional law, sanctioned legal tender status for Government paper money. The Court seemed guided more by expedience than principle, as justices in the majority drew upon the Constitution's highly elastic "necessary and proper clause" to validate paper money in wartime and other needful occasions (Siegan, 1984). In one Legal Tender Case, *Veazie Bank vs. Fenno*, the Supreme Court Chief Justice Salmon P. Chase was the same Chase who had earlier been Secretary of the Treasury when the Greenbacks were first issued. As a justice, Chase admitted his judgment had been clouded during the war. Upon reflection (in *Hepburn v. Griswold*, 1870), Chase argued that the Government did not have the right to issue paper money. But it was too late. The court eventually upheld the Legal Tender Act, thereby violating private property rights.

From the above it may be clear that the legal origin of the U.S. Government's modern authority to issue fiat paper money was not the Constitution or even the Federal Reserve Act of 1913, but a group of Supreme Court decisions after the Civil War. By 1913, the Government would obtain a complete monopoly on the issuance of money, albeit gold-convertible. Twenty years later, the U.S Federal Government (together with other governments around the world) would become a monopoly issuer of inconvertible fiat paper money. Thus, the Federal Reserve note is not the sole currency in the United States today because of its superior quality or because there exists some natural monopoly in money. It stems from a specific Government-granted monopoly on the issuance of money (Holzer, 1981a). Such grants of privilege — in this case a grant from Government to itself — clearly violate the private-property, limited Government system designed by America's Founding Fathers.

The Criminalization of Gold Ownership

In establishing a monopoly fiat paper dollar in 1933, the United States simultaneously outlawed private property rights to gold. Ownership was criminalized and the gold holdings of private citizens were confiscated. Those refusing to comply were subject to fines and jail terms (Holzer, 1981b). The U.S. Government simultaneously defaulted on the gold standard and reneged on the gold clauses in its bond contacts (Green, 1986). Widespread bank failures and the chaos of the Great Depression were used to justify these various steps. Gold and the gold standard were condemned as the root of all problems. This is a myth taken up in Chapter VI. Here it is enough to observe how much the legal status of gold and gold-based money deteriorated between ratification of the Constitution in 1789 and the anti-gold acts of 1933. Gold began as the premier market money, not to be tampered with by government, but ended up as a commodity the holding of which constituted criminal intent and a danger to society.

What brought about this change from the gold standard and freedom to fiat paper money and tyranny? As mentioned earlier, there were long episodes during the Middle Ages when gold and the pursuit of material wealth were seen as evil. An expanded church presence coincided with declining economic activity. The renewed suspicion of gold and free market money in the 1930s accompanied a growing array of statist interventions. Titles to gold were confiscated and replaced with grants of alleged "entitlements" to state welfare. Force had replaced gold as the standard. What might be the practical results of this substitution? As Ayn Rand observed:

> So long as men live together on earth and need means to deal with one another — their only substitute, if they abandon money, is the muzzle of a gun.... When force is the standard, the murderer wins over the pickpocket. And then that society vanishes, in a spread of ruins and slaughter. Do you wish to know when that day is coming? Watch money. Money is the barometer of a society's virtue. When you see that trading is done, not by consent, but by compulsion — when you see that in order to produce, you need to obtain permission from men who produce nothing — when you see that money is flowing to those who deal, not in goods, but in favors — when you see that men get richer by graft and by pull than by work, and your laws don't protect you against them, but protect them against you — when you see corruption being rewarded and honesty becoming a self-sacrifice — you may know that your society is doomed. Money is so noble a medium that it does not compete with guns and it does not make terms with brutality. It will not permit a country to survive as half-property, half-loot. (Rand, 1957, p. 413.)

The rise of the welfare state and the "mixed economy" — a mixture of freedom and controls — have dominated the post-Depression world. The producers increasingly were subordinated to the planners, just as money was subordinated to the state. Rand argued that any age dominated by statism also will be inimical to gold and free market money:

> Whenever destroyers appear among men, they start by destroying money, for money is men's protection and the base of a moral existence. Destroyers seize gold and leave to its owners a counterfeit pile of paper. This kills all objective standards and delivers men into the arbitrary power of an arbitrary setter of values. Gold was an objective value, an equivalent of wealth produced. Paper is a mortgage on wealth that does not exist, backed by a gun aimed at those who are expected to produce it. Paper is a check drawn by legal looters upon an account which is not theirs: upon the virtue of the victims. Watch for the day when it bounces, marked: "account overdrawn."... Until and unless you discover that money

is the root of all good, you ask for your own destruction. When money ceases to be the tool by which men deal with one another, then men become the tools of men. Blood, whips, and guns — or dollars. Take your choice — there is no other — and your time is running out. (Rand, 1957, 415.)

In this century, the regimes most hostile to gold and market money were most hostile to human freedom. Hitler, Stalin, and Mao each held to ideologies and policies that confiscated wealth, including its paramount symbol, gold. The policies of President Roosevelt were, in principle, no less confiscatory. President Nixon completed the confiscation in August 1971 by suspending the dollar's gold convertibility for foreign central banks, as President Roosevelt had done in 1933 for domestic U.S. citizens.

Since then, gold ownership in the United States has again been legalized (in 1975) and gold clauses again can be included in contracts (in 1977; see Holzer, 1980). However, the United States has not returned to anything resembling a gold standard or free banking. The United States still holds the bulk of the gold it first confiscated from the public in the 1930s. Most legal analysts doubt that gold clauses actually have the sanction of today's courts. Moreover, legal tender laws continue to grant a monopoly status to Government paper money. Under Gresham's law, bad money drives out good. That's still true today. Hence gold is no part of the modern monetary system, not because it is no longer economically fit to guide that system, but precisely because it is *more* fit than the paper dollar, while simultaneously treated in the law as equivalent in value to paper.

The breakdown in the political and legal framework of constitutional government has contributed to a breakdown of our money and banking system, and with it, our economic vitality.

VI.

SUBVERSION OF THE GOLD STANDARD

AFTER August 1914 the world never again enjoyed the degree of monetary freedom and unity it had experienced during the 19th century. The classical gold standard was the first casualty of World War I. Governments impaired and/or suspended the convertibility of their currencies during the war and thereafter depreciated them, before reconstructing monetary systems only marginally based on gold. The Great Depression and the worldwide economic disintegration of the 1930s reflected governments' purposeful destruction of the gold standard and other interventions. Nevertheless, these dire consequences of subverting the classical gold standard were, and remain, widely attributed to gold-based money, not to statism.

Throughout this century, governments gradually removed gold from their currencies and strengthened legal tender laws, forcing markets to use their currencies exclusively. By the end of 1971 all the world's currencies were completely severed from gold. Since 1971 there has been no "international monetary system" to speak of. Governments set their own "monetary policy" with unlimited discretion and an emphasis on their budgetary needs. The modern monetary landscape is strewn with an array of failed reforms and arcane treaties aimed at replicating the achievements of the classical gold standard while rejecting its key features. Modern money has been "balkanized."

The Monetary Dissolution of World War I

Gold's place in the monetary system changed drastically during and after World War I. Before the war, most gold was held as coin in private hands, currencies were fully convertible into gold, and the central banks that did exist refrained from active intervention. During and after the war, currency convertibility was suspended and gold came under government control. Governments seized gold coin from banks and individuals, melted coins into bullion in order to discourage demand, and replaced them with government paper money. According to one author, "appealing to patriotism, governments urged citizens to deposit any gold they possessed with the authorities. Of wartime experience, contemporaries said more gold was mined out of the pockets of the people than out of the mines of the earth" (Eichengreen, 1992). Governments hoarded gold and then immobilized it by setting minimum gold reserve requirements for central bank currency. Foreign exchange gradually displaced gold in the central banks' reserves. Government debts were monetized and currencies devalued. The U.S. Federal Reserve System adopted similar policies soon after it was established in 1913.

Officials and commentators at the time excused such changes as necessary to the effective conduct of war. Suspensions of convertibility were defended as a way to prevent adversaries from gaining a financial advantage. Gold had to be removed from private hands and hoarded by government as a show of financial strength, it was claimed. Unwilling to impose on taxpayers to finance war efforts, governments resorted to deficit spending, and insisted that central banks monetize their growing debts. During and after the war, "the preeminent concern of government officials was debt management," one historian explains. "So long as problems of debt management remained unresolved, governments were hesitant to restore to central banks the independence they had traditionally enjoyed. Central banks were pressured to keep discount rates low to minimize debt service costs and facilitate the placement of treasury issues" (Eichengreen, 1992, p. 105). Expedience overrode monetary integrity. In fact, a country's performance in war is worse with weaker currency, since it disrupts the economy. Sound money permits the sound conduct of war.

The Gold Exchange Standard

In the 4 decades prior to World War I, 59 countries had been on the classical gold standard. By 1919, most countries were issuing inconvertible, paper monies. Governments had not removed gold coin from the private sector in order to strengthen their currencies and ensure gold convertibility. Prices soared during the war. The ensuing sharp recession of 1920-21 convinced many officials and economists to seek a return to the prewar stability of the gold standard. That was the aim of an international monetary conference in Genoa in 1922. Unfortunately, countries did not return to the classical gold standard. The postwar monetary system depended more on paper than on gold.

Since at least the turn of the century central banks had begun to hold a growing proportion of each other's currencies as reserves. They began creating a pyramid of claims upon other claims. When the world's standard money was gold, this practice was not so dangerous. However, the practice accelerated after World War I. Now a pyramid of paper claims was built upon other paper claims. This system was called the *gold exchange standard*, even though gold played a much smaller role in its operation than did foreign exchange. By the late 1920s, the share of foreign exchange in international reserves was at least 50 percent above prewar levels. As exchange reserves grew quickly relative to monetary gold, the capacity of reserve countries, such as Britain, France and the United States, to maintain gold convertibility was cast into doubt. The gold exchange standard was prone to instability, reflecting instability in value of the inconvertible paper monies at its base and in the policies of the governments that issued them. Intervention, not gold, was to blame.

The gold exchange standard was not a product of free markets, but a deliberate policy to maximize governments' power to inflate money and finance the growing deficits that accompanied higher spending. The political-legal context necessary for a smooth-functioning gold standard was disintegrating. According to Eichengreen (1992), the turn of the century saw governments "unable to balance government budgets" to the point where "politicians enlisted the central bank's monetary printing presses to finance their deficits ... resulting in episodes of inflationary chaos and economic turmoil.... Issues that had previously remained outside the political sphere, such as the determination of wages and employment, suddenly became politicized" and "doubt was cast over the credibility of the commitment [to gold convertibility]." Speaking of the 19th century classical gold standard, he recounts how "convertibility provided a signal that a government's financial house was in order, and the gold standard inspired confidence on the part of domestic savers and investors." After World War I, "in an effort to maintain confidence, governments sought to disguise the extent of currency depreciation. They maintained convertibility de jure even when suspending it de facto." In other words, governments pursued a contradictory policy of "maintaining confidence" by cheating.

The gold exchange standard subordinated gold to statist goals. In the end, it was statism that sabotaged the classical gold standard.

Specific government interventions served to weaken the already flawed gold exchange standard. According to Eichengreen (1992), central banks "intervened systematically in the relationship between specie reserves and credit conditions," and "although licensing or prohibiting gold exports was inconsistent with laissez-faire principles, the war had taught officials to view such matters in a more pragmatic light." There was a "disintegration during and after WWI of the political and economic foundations of the prewar gold standard system" and "disputes over income distribution and the proper role for the state became increasingly contentious," while "economics and politics combined to challenge and ultimately compromise the independence of central bankers." Whereas "credibility and cooperation were central to the smooth operation of the classical gold standard, the scope of both declined abruptly with the intervention of World War I." He concludes by observing that "the interwar gold standard, despite resembling its prewar predecessor, shared few of these virtues" and "led a short and brutish life of barely 6 years (1925-1931)." These interventions set the stage for the U.S. stock market crash of 1929 and the worldwide Great Depression in the early 1930s.

Gold and the Great Depression

Prevailing economic folklore portrays the Great Depression and the severe monetary deflation that accompanied it as a failure of the gold standard. Eichengreen (1992) has argued that the gold standard shackled the international monetary system to an arbitrary commodity, thereby undermining economic stability: "The gold standard is conventionally portrayed as synonymous with financial stability," he writes, but "precisely the opposite was true. Far from being synonymous with stability, the gold standard itself was the principal threat to financial stability and economic prosperity between the wars." Why? Gold money is considered by Eichengreen and other critics as an impediment to prosperity because its supply cannot keep pace with the rate of economic growth. Thus a gold-based monetary system is considered to be prone to price deflation and ultimately — since wages do not fall with prices — unemployment. As employment declines, so does economic output; depression results. The gold standard is further criticized for shackling government policymakers who would otherwise be free to manage money and ensure full employment. In short, it is claimed that until and unless gold is abandoned in favor of government paper money, prosperity is elusive. As Eichengreen puts it:

> The gold standard fundamentally constrained the economic policies that government pursued. It was largely responsible for creating an unstable economic environment. The gold standard of the 1920s set the stage for the depression by heightening the fragility of the international financial system and was the mechanism transmitting destabilizing impulses from the U.S. to the rest of the world. It was the constraint preventing policy makers from averting the failure of banks and containing the spread of financial panic. Recovery proved possible, for these same reasons, only after abandoning the gold standard. (Eichengreen, 1992.)

This folklore about the gold standard and the Great Depression is mythical. The Great Depression was instigated not by adherence to sound money but by a *contravention* of sound money, by governments working actively to undermine the gold standard (Salsman, 1994a). The lesson of the Great Depression, still unlearned by the majority of economists today, is that sound money and free markets must not be tampered with. The gold exchange standard did not evolve from the free choice of private markets. It was a scheme built upon the shaky ground of government money and interventionism and lacked the self-regulating foundation of the market-based classical gold standard.

Government mismanagement of the gold standard leading up to the Great Depression can easily be pinpointed. When Britain returned to the gold standard in 1925, it did so at the exchange rate that prevailed before World War I, before a fivefold expansion of pound notes. The growth in pound notes during the war was inflationary. After the war, the number of pound note claims on gold far exceeded the supply of gold available to the

Bank of England to redeem them at the old rate. To sustain gold convertibility at this artificially high exchange rate without gold losses required a painful deflation of pound notes and prices. In order to help the Bank of England return to gold and prevent its gold stock from flowing abroad, the Federal Reserve pushed down U.S. interest rates, making Britain's rates relatively higher and encouraging Americans to hold claims to gold in pounds instead of dollars. The Fed's policy and the resulting increase in the foreign demand for pounds were to have offset the inflationary increase in their supply. Nevertheless, Britain suffered a contraction, as wages remained unduly elevated. Meanwhile, lower interest rates in the United States had stoked a speculative boom in securities. By 1929, the Fed's policy was reversed and rates were raised sharply. The U.S. stock market crashed later that year. Eventually, the United States suffered an economic contraction as severe as Britain's. The two countries that had achieved the most with gold money naturally suffered the most when it was sabotaged. By 1931, Britain once again suspended gold convertibility. As other countries followed, critics of the gold standard complained that there simply was not enough gold to go around.

The "Gold Shortage" Myth

What developed as a glut of government paper money during and after the war was misinterpreted as a basic shortage of physical gold by the 1930s. According to Eichengreen, a "slavish adherence to the gold standard" deprived the economy of liquidity, enslaved central banks, and deepened the contraction. This had to happen out of necessity, he asserts, because:

> The world supply of monetary gold is fixed at a moment in time.... [Central banks] engaged in desperate efforts to acquire gold from one another.... For the group as a whole, there was only so much gold to go around.... To defend the gold standard, the Fed refrained from engaging in expansionary open market operations ... Containing bank runs required policy makers to inject liquidity into the banking system, but this was inconsistent with the gold standard rules.... [So] the American money supply spiraled downward.... The dilemma was whether to sacrifice the gold standard in order to reflate, an option most policy makers continued to oppose, or to foreswear all measures that might stabilize the economy in order to defend the gold standard.... Far from being a bulwark of financial stability, the gold standard was the main impediment to its maintenance. (Eichengreen, 1992.)

In fact, there was no physical shortage of gold in the early 20th century, nor at any time before, and no limit to economic growth imposed by gold. The United States proved that in the 19th century. While it is true that the supply of gold virtually is "fixed" at any single point in time, this is irrelevant to the functioning of a gold standard. The key requirement is that a dollar or any other unit of account always hold its weight in gold and be convertible. If the value of the dollar is maintained, the market will create sufficient supplies of dollars required by the market. The supply of gold does not have to move in lockstep with production in the short run. In any event, the supply of gold grew at a rate of between 1 percent and 3 percent per year, even during the disruptions of World War I and the Great Depression. Meanwhile, the broader money supply, including bank demand deposits, fell by a third in the United States in the early 1930s. This deflating cannot be attributed to gold, especially since its supply was growing slowly. Nor were the world's central banks running short of gold before or during the Great Depression. On the contrary, the combined gold reserves of central banks increased more than 40 percent from 1927 to 1935.

In the 1930s, far from a gold famine, the world was suffering from a paper money glut as well as from the substitution of a gold exchange standard managed by politicians for the classical gold standard, managed by the market. Governments printed many more claims to gold during and after the war. There was an understandably unequal distribution of gold stock among central banks. Gold flowed to more financially stable countries, such as the United States and France, away from Germany and Britain. Those that inflated their currencies most, lost the most gold. Those that inflated least, gained gold. But the United States and France not only obtained gold due to financial prudence, they hoarded it in amounts beyond even the requirements of the gold exchange standard. For example, the Fed's gold reserve ratio was nearly twice the 40 percent minimum requirement in the 1930s. When the gold content of the dollar was reduced by 41 percent in March of 1933, the Federal Reserve was sitting atop a massive stockpile of gold. Ogden Mills, who had been Hoover's Secretary of the Treasury, remarked that "for a great central banking system to stand by with a 70 percent gold reserve without taking any active steps in such a situation was almost inconceivable and almost unforgivable" (Friedman and Schwartz, 1963, p. 385). The Federal Reserve was not blamed for its mismanagement of gold during the Great Depression, let alone forgiven for it. On the contrary, in 1935 the Fed was given more power to buy and sell Government securities and manipulate liquidity.

When Britain abandoned the gold standard in 1931, the pound was still a reserve currency for most of the world's other central banks. As the foreign exchange value of the pound plummeted, other central banks that held pounds suffered reserve losses and initiated further contractions of their own currencies. That development was unrelated to gold. Rather, it was the inevitable result of pyramiding paper upon paper. Markets valued gold more than pounds and dollars. From the time he was elected, FDR created uncertainty by hinting about a forthcoming devaluation, a diminution in the dollar's gold content. This encouraged the market to convert dollars into gold. Former U.S. Treasury Secretary Ogden Mills remarked in 1935 that "it was not the maintenance of the gold standard that caused the banking panic of 1933 and the outflow of gold ... it was the definite and growing fear that the new administration meant to do what they ultimately did — that is abandon the gold standard" (Eichengreen, 1992). Government intervention, not gold-based money, was to blame.

Other statist measures contributed to the Great Depression, such as the protectionism imposed by the Smoot-Hawley Act of 1930, the maintenance of artificially high wage rates by Government-supported labor unions, and the near doubling of income tax rates in the United States. The displacement of gold with Government money early in this century and the increased political manipulation of money since World War I account for the bulk of the monetary instabilities suffered in the 1930s.

Government Defaults on the Gold Standard

The U.S. Government defaulted on the gold exchange standard in March 1933, as Britain had done in September 1931. Other countries soon followed. The United States also repudiated the gold clauses in its bond indentures. France was the last major country to maintain gold convertibility, until finally it suspended in 1936. The major currencies of the world by then all were inconvertible claims. As discussed in Chapter V, these defaults under the gold exchange standard represented a violation of property rights. The violations had begun with the first interjections of forced government money, but the defaults of the 1930s represented brazen seizures. In hindsight, the rise and fall of gold was both glorious and tragic. Gold had begun and evolved as money. Then it was forcibly removed from the market and displaced with gold-convertible government money. Then governments defaulted on their commitments to pay gold and succeeded to some extent in confiscating remaining private holdings. Thus, in fewer than 3 decades in the early 20th century, what was once private gold was stolen from the world monetary system by governments all over the world.

A number of economists in the 1930s applauded this theft of gold from the monetary system. Some contended that the Great Depression was resolved in part by defaulting on the gold exchange standard. Soon after Britain's default in 1931, economist John Maynard Keynes wrote of:

> The great advantages to British trade and industry of our ceasing artificial efforts to maintain our currency above its real value were quickly realized. *There are few Englishman who do not rejoice at the breaking of our gold fetters.* We feel that we have at last a free hand to do what is sensible. The romantic phase is over, and we can begin to discuss realistically what policy is for the best.... The competitive disadvantage will

71

be concentrated on those few countries which remain on the gold standard. On these will fall the curse of Midas. (Keynes, 1932.)

Eichengreen (1992) concurs with Keynes and argues that countries abandoning gold earliest also recovered earliest. "Currency depreciation stimulated economic recovery," he argues. "Prices were stabilized in countries that went off gold. Output, employment, investment and exports rose more quickly than in countries that clung to gold." He says "only when principles of orthodox finance were abandoned did recovery follow" because "in the absence of gold standard restraints, international cooperation was no longer essential," thereby "permitting more expansionary monetary and fiscal policies...." Such claims lack supporting evidence. Industrial production was starting to turn up in the United States in 1932, a year before devaluation. Moreover, in 1937-38 the United States suffered another, although milder, depression. Industrial production fell 12 percent. The unemployment rate was 19 percent in 1938, higher than it had been in 1931. In fact, most of the world remained mired in recession until after World War II.* And contrary to the optimism expressed by Keynes in the wake of Britain's default, that once-great country never did regain its prewar economic stature. The resort to inconvertible paper money was a sign of weakness, not of strength. Prosperity could not be printed.

The gold standard cannot be held accountable for the Great Depression. The real culprit was statism, which had grown more pronounced since the turn of the century. The "progressive era" in the United States saw an expansion of government power, symbolized by the introduction of a new Federal income tax (1916) and a new central bank (1913). Similar trends took hold globally. The first full-fledged welfare state was instituted under Bismarck in Germany in the 1880s. As the late economist Melchior Palyi argued, it was "an age of monetary and commercial nationalism, with the central banks of the world at the mercy of political forces. The welfare state's determination to bypass the automatic workings of the gold standard resulted in making the gold standard unworkable" (1972). Statism meant a vast expansion of government into hitherto private economic affairs, a trend shaped by critics of gold such as John Maynard Keynes. In 1936 Keynes looked favorably on the breakdown of gold and free trade and applauded the return of the mercantilist-nationalist policies that had predated Adam Smith:

The mercantilists were under no illusions as to the nationalistic character of their policies, but intellectually, their realism is much preferable to the

---

* Recovery came not from war spending itself, as traditional interpretations contend, but by the postwar return to a form of gold money under the Bretton Woods system (1944), a reduction in tax rates, the removal of many protectionist impediments via the GATT treaty, industry deregulation, and conversion to civilian production.

confused thinking of contemporary advocates of an internationally fixed gold standard and laissez-faire, who believe that it is precisely these policies which will best promote peace. (Keynes, 1936, p. 348.)

Economic and monetary nationalism did not solve the depression, as Keynesians would claim, but made it possible. Indeed, nationalism and the gold standard are incompatible. Gold is worldwide, international money, objectively valued, and freely accepted by all. Government paper is arbitrary and imposed on markets by force. Any interpretation of the interwar period should be consistent with what is known to have occurred before and after it. The interwar period was a mixture of laissez-faire and interventionism. Before World War I, governments and central banks were relatively limited, major countries had no central banks, the gold standard worked well, and economies prospered. In the decades since World War I, new central banks were established and all central banks grew more beholden to governments that grew more interventionist. Available evidence supports the conclusion that the gold standard was made a scapegoat for the Great Depression, for the failures of government intervention in money. Yet intervention is greater today than ever. Economic instability, inflating, financial crises, and currency protectionism now are commonplace. Central bank "independence" from government, while seen as a necessity and a virtue, is nevertheless a myth.

The Bretton Woods System and Its Aftermath

Economic recovery from the contraction of the 1930s was slow. When it came, it was not brought about by defaults on the gold exchange standard or by governments spending billions in armaments during World War II, as is often asserted (Eichengreen, 1992). On the contrary, monetary devaluations and wars have tended to cheapen money and undermine wealth creation, not boost it. Markets function best in peacetime and with a money that holds a relatively constant purchasing power. That is the reason gold first became the money of choice and why gold-based money not manipulated by government has delivered the best economic performance. Government currencies, in contrast, have been prone to inflating and deflating. The German hyperinflation of 1922-23 and the U.S. deflation of 1930-34 are only extreme examples of this tendency. Less severe swings in money's value also are disruptive, although to a lesser degree.

When governments force unstable money on people, markets suffer. Gyrating prices and interest rates give mixed and confusing signals. When government monetary intervention ceases or at least diminishes, markets tend to improve. One source of deflation in the 1930s had been a sharply rising demand for dollar currency in order to retrieve gold, coupled with a flight from bank (checking deposit) money. People trusted gold money, not the money of the U.S. Government nor of its highly regulated unit banking system. When gold was abandoned, citizens had no choice remaining but to accept government paper money and hence no opportunity to seek gold in place of paper. Thus the paper dollar deflation subsided to some degree. This is why economies appear to have stabilized for a while in the later 1930s, after gold was abandoned. Market's need credible money. This only reinforces the case for gold-based private money and fully protected property rights.

The only sustainable economic expansion after the Great Depression was achieved when gold was reintroduced in the international monetary system, albeit in diluted form, under the Bretton Woods agreement of 1944. Like its interwar predecessor, Bretton Woods was a gold exchange standard, albeit in even more diluted form. Better described as a "dollar exchange standard," Bretton Woods pegged the world's currencies to gold only indirectly. The dollar was defined as 1/35 of an ounce of gold, the equivalent of a gold price of $35/ounce and the U.S. Government committed to exchanging dollars for gold at that rate. Other currencies were pegged to the dollar. Thus fixed exchange rates were reestablished. Paper dollars were used more extensively as reserves by foreign central banks.

Bretton Woods departed from earlier gold standards in a number of critical ways. Gold was held by central banks and in bullion form, not by citizens in coin form. And the commitment of the United States to pay gold was made only to foreign central banks, not to U.S. citizens. Often that commitment went unmet, as diplomatic pressure was applied to prevent gold withdrawals from the United States. Devaluations and controls on capital and gold flows persisted. Britain devalued twice under Bretton Woods. Other countries devalued more often. Some major currencies were not even linked to the dollar until 1958. Thus in a number of critical features, the strict discipline of a classical gold coin standard was absent.

The weaknesses in this "dollar exchange" system as compared to the classical gold standard are apparent. The United States could inflate the supply of dollars and see them pile up as reserves in the vaults of other central banks. It could run perpetual balance of payments deficits. Bretton Woods centralized the monetary system even more so than the financial policies of World War I, for now the money of only one country (the United States) was the hub of all other monetary systems. The core of the international monetary system was not the credibility of gold money but the credibility of the U.S. Government. In 1961, U.S. President John F. Kennedy described what was required of the United States to maintain this system:

> The growth in foreign dollar holdings has placed upon the United States
> a special responsibility — that of maintaining the dollar as the principal
> reserve currency of the free world. This required that the dollar be con-

sidered by many countries to be as good as gold. It is our responsibility to sustain this confidence. (Cited in Weber, 1988.)

Lofty rhetoric aside, the United States did not keep the dollar "as good as gold." It could not hope to do so, given its own explicitly chosen Keynesian policies of deficit spending and inflating. Within a decade of Kennedy's speech, the United States defaulted on the dollar exchange standard. The Kennedy and Johnson administrations set the United States on a course of sustained deficit spending and inflating unprecedented in the Nation's history. The last balanced budget was in 1969. The United States lost vast amounts of gold. During the entire Bretton Woods era (1947-71), the U.S. gold stock fell by more than 50 percent, from 653 million ounces to only 296 million ounces, mostly during the Kennedy and Johnson years (Weber, 1988). In March 1965, the gold reserve requirement against the Federal Reserve banks' deposit liabilities was eliminated, as was gold backing for Federal Reserve notes in March 1968. That same month, the London "gold pool" disbanded and central banks stopped making their currencies convertible at $35/ounce.

The United States was not the only country inflating under Bretton Woods. Other countries did so as well. As foreign central banks used dollars as reserves, they complained of a "dollar shortage," just as they had complained of gold shortages under the gold exchange standard. The more removed the monetary system was from gold, the more paper money was printed and the less governments in the system seemed able to see that the real problem was paper, not gold. To address the alleged shortages of gold and dollars, in 1970 governments established a bookkeeping entry, titled Special Drawing Rights, or SDRs, with the intergovernmental Bank for International Settlements. Dubbed "paper gold" at the time, SDRs were a brazen attempt to practice modern alchemy. The SDR program is based on the old myth that there is "not enough gold." Still used today, SDRs represent the "contributions" made by participating governments (by taxing their citizens) into a common fund. The world's financial deadbeats "draw" their sustenance from the SDR fund. Since few draws ever are fully repaid, new contributions continually are required — from the wealthiest nations. SDRs are the farthest thing from gold one could imagine. That central banks could imagine they could create such fictions and call them gold is a sign of how removed they are from the practical workings of markets.

The creation of SDRs neither created gold nor did anything to solve the real problem of excessive paper money creation and its result — worldwide price inflation. If anything, SDRs contributed to it by creating more paper claims instead of more wealth. The United States went on losing gold after SDRs were created. From 1968 onward, the United States actively tried to resist foreign government demands for gold convertibility solely

75

through political persuasion. For a while, it seemed to work, but when France objected to the holding of dollars it did not trust any longer and demanded payment in gold, President Nixon responded in August 1971 by "closing the gold window," a polite expression for defaulting on gold payments and repudiating an international monetary agreement. This default was not substantially different from the "third world" debt defaults that would later take place in the 1980s. The U.S. gold default of 1971 was the act of a banana republic. The U.S. dollar has been unhinged from gold ever since.

By 1971, more than half of the gold supply that was forcibly taken from U.S. citizens in the 1930s ended up in the vaults of foreign central banks. This was the biggest bank heist in world history. It happened in slow motion and may not have been the intent of every official who participated in it. But that was the result and many officials and economists actually applauded the abandonment of gold money at every step.

Despite the breakdown of the dollar-gold link in the Bretton Woods system, the global lending agencies that had been established under the system remained in existence and even expanded after 1971. The World Bank and the International Monetary Fund originally were established to make the Bretton Woods system operational — to help countries "manage" their balance of payments in order to stay on the dollar exchange standard. When the link between the dollar and gold was broken in 1971, there technically no longer was a need for these agencies. But as with all government bureaucracies, they fought to stay in place. They contributed to the "third world" lending crisis of the following decade by guaranteeing loans to uncreditworthy governments for state projects. These agencies, funded as they are by the taxpayers of industrialized countries, continue to transfer wealth from producers to nonproducers.

When gold was "demonetized" in 1971, many critics of gold predicted that its price would fall below $35/ounce. They assumed that the paper dollar gave value to gold, not the other way around. Unlike J. P. Morgan, they did not know that gold was money. But in the decade after the gold-defined dollar was abandoned, the price of gold headed upward. In other words, the paper dollar plummeted in value. In January 1980, the dollar price of gold moved above $800 per ounce. Price inflation and interest rates reached double digits (see Chart 7). A "dollar crisis" rocked foreign exchange markets. World economies lurched into recession. What did this record-high gold price mean? According to government officials, nothing in the least (Levine and Janssen, 1980). Federal Reserve Board Governor Henry Wallich referred to activity in the gold market as a "side show." Savers and bondholders lost billions, as Wallich echoed the views of the late British economist John Maynard Keynes, that the gold standard was a relic and gold was of consequence to no one but speculators and cranks.

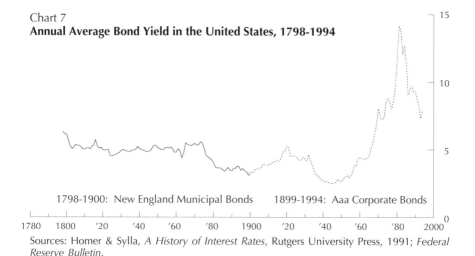

Chart 7
Annual Average Bond Yield in the United States, 1798-1994

1798-1900: New England Municipal Bonds   1899-1994: Aaa Corporate Bonds

1780   1800   '20   '40   '60   '80   1900   '20   '40   '60   '80   2000

Sources: Homer & Sylla, *A History of Interest Rates*, Rutgers University Press, 1991; *Federal Reserve Bulletin*.

Markets and other observers saw things differently. According to one commentator, developments in the gold market were no "side show," but, rather, "a highly sensitive scoreboard for the main event" (Lehrman, 1980). What event? An open forum on the value of real money. The dollar was losing badly to gold.

Despite its inefficiencies and injustices, the Bretton Woods system nevertheless proved superior to the purely fiat paper money systems that preceded it (1934-44) and followed it (1971 to the present). Between 1947 and 1971, according to figures calculated by Salsman (1994b), real GDP in the United States grew an average of 3.5 percent per year. Productivity grew 3.5 percent yearly. The average rate of price inflation was only 2.6 percent. Real wages grew an average of 1.8 percent. Unemployment averaged 4.7 percent. Treasury bond yields averaged 3.8 percent. This performance has deteriorated dramatically since 1971. From the abandonment of gold money in 1971 through the end of 1993, real GDP grew an average of only 2.6 percent yearly and productivity by only 1.4 percent. Real wages have *fallen* an average of 0.5 percent per year and the average annual price inflation rate has doubled to 5.2 percent, unemployment has averaged 6.5 percent, and Treasury bond yields have more than doubled to average 8.6 percent. Since 1971 the dollar price of gold has risen more than tenfold, which means the paper dollar in terms of real money has fallen to one-tenth of its previous value. The dollar has fallen from 360 yen in 1971 to below 90 yen more recently. The last balanced budget in the United States was recorded in 1969. Since that time, Government spending, tax revenues, and debt have all skyrocketed. Those wishing to reform this budgetary profligacy generally leave unquestioned the Government's fiat paper money monopoly.

Just as the quality of money has deteriorated in the quarter century since

Bretton Woods broke down, so has the quality of banking, especially in the United States (Salsman, 1990). In the 1980s, U.S. bank failures reached levels unseen since the Great Depression. Bank capital ratios spiraled downward. The U.S. Federal deposit insurance fund, established in 1934 to bolster bank safety, only promoted bank recklessness by charging flat-rate premiums, bailing out the most imprudent banks and raising taxes on the more conservative survivors. By 1991, the fund was depleted (Salsman, 1993). Yet many economists blamed this on bank "deregulation," not on fiat paper money or Government intervention.

Recent Failed Attempts at Unified Money

The subversion of the gold standard in this century has accompanied a subversion of currency stability and economic prosperity. Monetary re-formers have searched for ways to reunify the world's money ever since it was torn asunder in 1971, but these have been attempts to fix floating paper money values against one another. The Smithsonian Agreement (since abandoned), the European Monetary System (since abandoned), and the proposed Maastricht Treaty all were attempts to achieve stability in exchange rates, but without any reference whatsoever to gold. Some econo-mists, especially the supply-siders, have begun to look back on the classi-cal gold standard with renewed interest and respect. Occasionally some official suggests that the price of gold might serve as "an independent reference point" in gauging policy, but such mentions of gold are quickly dismissed by other officials. International monetary reformers today are flailing about in a sea of fiat paper money, intent on ignoring the evidence that the only monetary anchor worth its weight is gold.

The failure of today's fiat paper systems to replicate the success of the classical gold standard should serve to demonstrate the latter's superiority. When the European Monetary System unraveled in September 1992, its failure was attributed to the attempt to fix exchange rates at all, a feature that is now but a pale vestige of a real gold standard. One article in *The Economist*, "The Gold Standard Revisited," blamed the breakdown of the EMS on gold, even though gold is nowhere to be found in today's mon-etary system. This overwhelming bias against gold is our true modern burden. These modern-day failures to unify money stem from the failure of statism, a failure many economists still are unwilling to acknowledge, at least in money and banking. Mainstream economists remain united against fixed exchange rates. Keynesian critics oppose them because they want no diminution in government discretion over money. Monetarists are critics as well, alleging that fixed exchange rates amount to *government price-fixing*. Monetarists fail to recognize that a dollar defined as a fixed weight of gold is an *identity*, or a standard, not a state dictate. A gold standard no more involves "price fixing" than does the Government's definitions of the

78

quarter, dime, or nickel vis-à-vis the dollar, or weights and measures at the Bureau of Standards. Floating exchange rates are *not* equivalent to a "free market" approach in currencies, especially when such currencies are the nationalized products of states.

Attempts to link currencies, although well-intentioned, are futile without gold. As long as governments are interventionist, protectionist, and prone to deficit spending they will rely heavily on central banking, inflating, and devaluations. Such policies are inimical to fixed exchange rate systems of any kind, let alone those based on gold. Thus none of the non-gold systems tried since 1971 have succeeded. No future fixed-exchange rate system established without gold can long succeed, either.

VII.

CENTRAL BANKING AND GOLD

W HAT role has central banking played in the rise and fall of gold money? Did central banks "orchestrate" the highly successful classical gold standard of the 19th century, as Eichengreen (1987) contends? Or were they passive participants? Were central banks responsible for the downfall of the gold standard in the 20th century? Or did gold money fail on its own account? What has been the record of central banking without gold backing? Why do governments continue to hold gold, having long-since abandoned the gold convertibility of their currencies? Why do legal restrictions on the private use of gold persist? One cannot begin to answer these questions without first understanding the purpose of central banking.

Central Banking: A Form of Central Planning

No government today is without a central bank. That was not true a century ago, when central banks did not yet exist, for example, in Switzerland, Canada or the United States. Those that did exist a century ago, such as the Bank of England and the German Reichsbank, had limited powers. Today, central banks have inordinate power and privilege, courtesy of their sponsoring governments. Central banks today are first and foremost the monopoly issuers of standard, legal tender money in their respective countries. Private banks issue checking deposit money, but these accounts must be convertible into government paper money. Additionally, central banks are a placement agent for government debt securities, buying and selling them through the banking system. Central banks also buy government debt directly, a process referred to as "monetization," which amounts to creating money out of thin air. Central banks are above all bankers to government. The bulk of their assets is comprised of loans to governments.

Central banks also record massive profits from their privileged positions. How? They receive interest income from the government securities they hold. In turn, they have few expenses because their main liability is noninterest-bearing inconvertible paper money. Central bank "profits," which are not earned by providing any valuable product or service in the private sector, are always paid over to government (Timberlake, 1986). For example, the Federal Reserve recorded revenues in excess of expenses of approximately $25 billion in 1994, more than the entire private banking system will earn. The Fed will have done so by lending almost exclusively to the U.S. Government. The so-called profits of central banks clearly are not earned in a competitive environment. Central banking entails a monopoly on money and a legal prohibition against privately issued standard money.

Central banks serve as a "lender of last resort" not only to government but to select private firms deemed "too big to fail" without disrupting the monetary system. Central banks sometimes will guarantee loans of other countries, through international monetary agencies such as the World Bank and the IMF. Central banks intervene in foreign exchange markets, manipulate the value of money, interest rates, and the business cycle. They also have a regulatory apparatus that intervenes in private banking decisions. Most countries have government deposit insurance systems as well, which tend to subsidize imprudent banking practices. Central banks today conduct their policies with few limitations imposed by government and with no independent discipline, such as gold convertibility. These are the unlimited powers of central banking and its auxiliary agencies.

Economics textbooks today describe central banks as "managing" the economy, controlling interest rates, smoothing business cycles, "fighting" inflation, fostering job growth, and regulating the safety and soundness of banks. There is little evidence that any of this is so. Since the establishment of central banking, especially in the United States (in 1913), interest rates and business cycles have been more volatile, unemployment rates have been higher, and banking has been less prudent (Salsman, 1990).

Not surprisingly, textbooks often couple their support of central banking with the claim that, left to its own devices, a free economy — including a free banking system based on gold — is prone to wide swings in the business cycle, to bouts of price inflation and deflation, to foreign supply "shocks" and unemployment, to bank frauds and failures. Central banking and its related apparatus — Federal deposit insurance and bank regulatory agencies — are said to provide the solution to these alleged market failures. Best-selling textbook writer and MIT economist Paul Samuelson has regaled his student readers with such tales since at least 1948, when he wrote that central banking was established in the United States in 1913 because "the country was fed up once and for all with the anarchy of unstable, private banking." In his chapter on money and banking, Samuelson wrote:

> Certainly if one reviews the history of private, small scale nineteenth century banking, there is plenty of gloom to be found in it…. All countries have long recognized that banking is one of those activities 'affected with a public interest' and in need of government control. They have created central banks, like the Federal Reserve System and the Bank of England, to correct the inherent instability of laissez-faire banking…. How is government action able to bring important change, without which our system of small unit banking would remain perilously unsafe?… The government can (and must!) use its *boundless emergency monetary powers* to avert collapse whenever a real financial crisis should arise…. Without government regulation and examination, without the Federal Reserve System,

and without guaranteeing of bank deposits by the FDIC, our system of small unit banking would be intolerable. (Samuelson, 1948, pp. 322-323.)

Samuelson's scorn for free banking and adulation for central banking are not based on fact. U.S. banking practices were more prudent before central banking and deposit insurance were established than afterward. What people were "fed up" with in 1913 were the frequent currency shortages that arose because Government policy prevented banks from issuing currency not backed by Government debt. That policy was aimed not at promoting free markets or sound currency, but at securing Government funds. Instabilities did arise from this intervention as well as from "unit banking" laws, which brought a proliferation of one-office banks. "Unit banking," an intentional government policy that prevented banks from branching and diversifying, was enacted to hinder the development of large banks. This was hardly consistent with laissez-faire banking. Unit banking laws were responsible in part for the wave of bank failures in the 1930s and for nearly all the bank failures in Texas (which retained unit banking laws) in the 1980s. Yet Samuelson mistakenly attributes problems arising from interventionism to freedom. His opposition to free banking and support for central banking and deposit insurance never diminished in later editions of his famous text, despite facts to the contrary.

Central banking is not in place today because free markets in money and banking failed. There was no such failure. Banking's historical instabilities have resulted from government intervention in banking. Why then has there been such intervention in the first place? What is the basic purpose of central banking? The intimate connection that exists between central banking, government expansion, and central planning offers a clue. Central banking is nothing but central planning applied to money and banking. It is no part of a genuine free-market economy. Central bankers themselves seem aware of this. Paul Volcker, Chairman of the Federal Reserve from 1979 to 1986, has observed that:

Central banks are not exactly the harbingers of free market economies.... As I began looking at the central banks in the Western world, I realized they were not at the cutting edge of a market economy.... With a few exceptions ... central banking is almost entirely a phenomenon of the twentieth century. And there were market economies long before the twentieth century. Indeed, to some extent, *central banks were looked upon and created as a means of financing the government,* which I do not think people have in mind when they think about central banking today.... If you say a central bank is essential to a market economy, I have to ask you about Hong Kong, which has no central bank at all in the absolute epitome of a free market economy. Yet it does quite well in terms of economic growth and stability. (Volcker, 1990, emphasis added.)

A closer look at how central banking was first established and how it evolved makes clear what Volcker is referring to. There are many good histories of central banking. Charles Goodhart, a monetary economist at the Bank of England from 1968 to 1985 and fervid defender of central banking, has offered a history of the evolution of all modern central banks (1985). In nearly every instance, he found that central banks were not established to correct market failure but to permit government access to the banking system it would not otherwise have. According to Goodhart:

> When the first government-sponsored banks were founded in Europe, for example the Swedish Riksbank (1668) and the Bank of England (1694), there was no intention that these should undertake the functions of a modern central bank, that is, discretionary monetary management and regulation ... Instead, the initial impetus was much more basic, generally relating to *the financial advantages a government felt it could obtain from the support of such a bank* ... This naturally involved some favoritism, often supported by legislation, by the government for this particular bank in return for its financial assistance. The favored bank was often granted a monopoly advantage, for example over the note issue in certain areas, or as the sole chartered joint stock bank in the country; and this may have had the effect in some countries, such as England and France, of weakening the early development of other commercial banks. (Goodhart, 1987, emphasis added.)

The origin and the evolution of central banking does not show governments fixing "market failure," but rather governments co-opting private banking systems and confiscating wealth. A history of the Bank of England indicates that the bank was established in 1694 to help pay for a war with France. Prior to that time, the British monarchy simply raided private gold holdings. For example, early in the 17th century,

> It became the practice of the citizens of London to lodge their surplus coin and bullion at the Mint in the Tower of London. This practice continued until 1640 when the confidence of the London merchants in the Tower as a place where their gains might be deposited with safety was rudely shaken, for the King, failing in his attempts to raise money by grants from Parliament or by means of levies, ordered the treasure of the merchants to be seized. Vigorous protests resulted in the money being returned on condition that 40,000 pounds was lent to the King, but after such an occurrence it became obvious to the merchants that the Tower could not be regarded as a safe depository ... (Acres, 1931, p. 4.)

Advisors to William III lobbied for a government bank in England soon after the Revolution of 1688, in part to avoid the bad publicity associated with such naked raids on wealth. According to one author, the crown's efforts to oppose France "necessitated an increased revenue, which, in consequence of the divided state of the nation, it was difficult to raise, though many new taxes were imposed ... The Ministers of the Crown frequently found it necessary to borrow money ... at a high rate of interest ... and it was for the credit and security of the government, rather than any advantage which might accrue to the trading community, that the friends of the new Constitution advocated the establishment of a national Bank ... The Act [to establish the Bank of England in 1694] was only passed to avoid embarrassment to the Government, which needed the money immediately, and could not obtain it otherwise" (Acres, 1931, pp. 7, 11). Thus the monarchy's raids on British wealth continued, albeit disguised in a new government borrowing scheme and a central bank.

Goodhart (1988) concurs with Acres's history of the Bank of England. He also concedes that central banks exist primarily to secure for government some nontax form of revenue, that "such confiscation is, perhaps most easily achieved by monopolizing the note issue in a Central Bank" (p. 21). Goodhart has provided details on the origins of today's major central banks. The first central bank, the Swedish Riksbank, was formed in 1668 after the government nationalized a failed private bank. But that bank was "private" in name only; indeed it had failed because it was primarily a lender to the Swedish government. When the government defaulted on its loans, it simply took over the bank in order to retain an on-going source of financing. Government favoritism, not a failure of free markets, explains the world's first central bank. The Riksbank grew in step with the growth of government.

Other central banks also were formed to serve government. According to Goodhart, the German Reichsbank was established in 1875 and had been "founded along the model of, and indeed quite largely by taking over, the Prussian State Bank, and this had been founded and functioned primarily as a state bank to further the financial interests of Prussia." The bank's role grew in the 1880s when the world's first cradle-to-grave welfare state was being established under Bismarck. Goodhart tells us that "the government could always, when it really needed to, call the tune" regarding policy at the Reichsbank. While the bank delivered seignorage profits to government, it "sought to place legal restrictions on private banks." From the turn of the century onward, "the Reichsbank was very liberal in extending credits" and in 1922-23 sponsored the world's most notorious hyperinflation. The Swiss central bank was established in 1905 for reasons that "were much the same as in the instance of the Reichsbank."

The central bank in France was established in 1800 by Napoleon, Goodhart explains, because "the Treasury needed money ... he could not get what he wanted from the free banks ... [and he] wanted to have under his hand an establishment which he could compel to meet his wishes." As Napoleon put it, "I have created the Bank in order to allow a discount of 4%," a sub-market rate at that time. By 1805 he had removed all gold from the bank to finance his military campaigns and by 1848 the bank enjoyed a complete monopoly on currency issuance. The Bank of Italy was formed in 1844 when a private bank was granted an exclusive right to issue currency. Shortly, "this bank became the government's bank, providing large loans to the government, in return for which the government in 1866 freed the bank from the obligation of redeeming notes in specie ..." The Bank of Japan was formed in 1882 for similar reasons. In all of these countries, central banking was established to finance government and grew hand-in-hand with government. Where necessary, central banks simply overrode or undermined the interests of private banks and their customers.

The Federal Reserve was established in 1913 to prevent instabilities that were attributed to the private banking system. However, the occasional money panics and currency shortages in the decades after the Civil War were due to Government restrictions on bank branching and currency issuance, not to free markets. Limits on branching limited loan and deposit diversification and unnecessarily weakened private banks. In addition, private banks were required by law to back their currency by Government debt, a leftover from a policy designed to help the Government finance the Civil War. When the national debt was paid down during the decades after the war, the supply of bank currency was not allowed to expand and contract with the needs of trade. Nor could the composition of money — checking deposits versus currency — freely be altered. Yet this was an era of rapid industrialization and growth in the United States and of growing demand for money to circulate in production and trade. It was this corset of government controls, not a free banking market, that proved destabilizing. After the panic of 1907, people agitated for an "elastic" currency." Instead of repealing its own legal restrictions on private money and banking, Government blamed private bankers and nationalized the currency. This continued a pattern in U.S. history of introducing a new intervention in the monetary system to fix the problems and distortions created by previous interventions (Salsman, 1993b).

Historians of the theory of central banking concur with the historical record examined by Goodhart. Vera Smith (1990), for example, finds that "an examination of the reasons for the eventual decision in favor of central banking as opposed to a free banking system reveals in most countries a combination of political motives and historical accident which played a much more important part than any well-considered economic principle" (pp. 4-5). In other words, there is no economic justification for central banking. There is no so-called "natural monopoly" in money, no supportable argument that a single, monopoly issuer of money provides the highest-quality and most efficient outcome (Vaubel, 1984). Politics — the support of government — is central banking's only reason for being.

Over the centuries, the kinds of government operations in most need of central bank financing have changed. The earliest central banks tended to be formed at times of war when government did not want to overtax a citizenry from which it expected patriotic support. Central banks still tend to inflate during wartime today. However, in the past century they expanded to support the massive deficit-spending associated with the welfare state. Central banking powers have expanded though most of the 20th century, together with the expansion of deficit spending, welfare functions, and central planning.

Central banks have never relinquished their first and most important role of financing government. Today the assets of every central bank consist almost entirely of loans made to sponsoring governments and gold initially seized from the private sector. Central banks now do more than underwrite government loans and generate nontax revenues. They conduct "monetary policy." They expand and contract the money supply, manipulate interest rates and credit, and regulate the major decisions of private banks (lending, branching, pricing, merging with other banks). Governments have turned central banks into central planning vehicles with the ostensive purpose of controlling the business cycle, fighting inflation, maximizing employment, and ensuring safe and sound banking.

The record of central banking in these areas has been poor. Economic growth has been lower and money less stable under central banking. This should be no surprise. Central banking is just another form of central planning, applied to money and banking. Central planning has failed wherever it has been tried, because it constitutes the use of force in otherwise voluntary human affairs. When people are forced to do what they would not otherwise do, they will not deliver the economic coordination and prosperity that freedom delivers (and planners only promise). Central planning has "succeeded" only in throttling economic efficiency and production and replacing it with stagnation and poverty. In the same sense, central banking has tended to ruin the quality of money and banking (Salsman, 1990). As Economist Lawrence White (1993) explains:

> When we assign the production of money to government, we should expect inferior money. I see no reason to think that money production differs from mail delivery in this regard. Even if a government agency could be assigned a coherent and desirable quality objective, the problem of accountability or enforcement remains. Particularly with government of the current size and scope, the political process simply does not enable citizens-consumers to hold a government agency tightly accountable for a poor-quality product. Once we take the accountability problem seriously, we should ... recognize that the best real cure for monetary instability lies in abolishing the Federal Reserve System's money-creating

powers. To propose that monetary policy can be harnessed to a single clear and measurable objective is to engage in wishful thinking given the logic of political bureaucracies. (White, 1993, p. 191.)

Central banking has "succeeded" in only one function, in its original function, as the financier of gigantic government. Central banks are bankers to unlimited governments, governments that spend more than they have been able or willing to levy in taxes on the populace. The advantages of being able to avoid paying for expanded government by taxing voters are obvious. The disruptive effects of such intervention, such as price inflation or reckless banking, can be blamed on "greedy" businessmen and bankers. Constitutionally limited and creditworthy governments do not need central banks. They are able to finance their operations in a free market with ready access to the private credit system.

The Incompatibility of Central Banking and the Gold Standard

Some economic historians who blame the gold standard for the Great Depression nevertheless have credited central banking with the smooth operation of the 19th century classical gold standard. Eichengreen has described the classical gold standard as an "orchestra" that was conducted by the Bank of England (1987). Elsewhere he describes central banks as "the traditional guardians of the gold standard"(1992, xi). "The stability of the prewar gold standard," he insists, was the result of central bank credibility, "the confidence invested by the public in the government's commitment to a policy.... In the prewar period there was little doubt that the authorities ultimately would take whatever steps were required to defend the central bank's reserves and maintain the convertibility of the currency into gold" (p. 5). These steps included lending to one another when there were gold losses, adjusting interest rates to accommodate each other in times of stress. In effect, central bank actions were geared to assisting the gold standard instead of overriding it. Importantly, "rather than advocating active monetary management to stabilize the economy, the majority of observers advised a passive and therefore more predictable monetary stance" (p. 6). Had central banks not cooperated, Eichengreen says, the gold standard would have broken down. When international cooperation did break down during the war, so did the gold standard. In Eichengreen's estimation, the classical gold standard, epitome of a laissez-faire age, could not survive without careful central bank nurturing.

How much evidence, if any, supports this assessment? The smooth operation of the classical gold standard embodied the customs, standards, and rules that markets had adopted over the centuries. These rules were widely respected, fostered credibility, and lent stability to the monetary system. That all changed with the advent of central banking and government intervention in money, especially during World War I. As we have seen, central banks impeded gold flows, turned coin into bullion, discouraged domestic convertibility, and hoarded gold. Central banks then added to the instability by raising and lowering interest rates at will, above and below market rates, to manipulate trade flows and the domestic business cycle. In short, as Nurske (1944) shows, they broke all the rules. A study by Bloomfield (1959) for the Federal Reserve Bank of New York demonstrates that central banks began manipulating the gold standard even before World War I. Palyi has observed that:

> Until about 1870, the prevailing approach of central banks consisted in following the trend of the money market rather than in trying to influence it — in brief, taking no initiative whatsoever. The absence of an active policy was justified by the alleged inability of central bank managements to resist the market forces. [But there developed a] dissatisfaction with this comfortable abstinence ... A new approach developed under the leadership of the Bank of England in the late 1860s and early 1870s.... The practice of central banking had now evolved to the use of discretionary measures — that is, as far as 'control' over short-term fluctuations in the balance of payments and in domestic credit conditions was concerned. (Palyi, 1972, pp. 14-18.)

There was no problem with the gold standard's automatic functioning. Governments and their central banks simply could not leave it alone. The problem was the growth of government and nationalist-protectionist sentiments. Trade deficits were considered wrong. Accordingly, central banks tried to manipulate money markets to prevent the gold outflows necessary to pay for deficits. Domestically, central banks took it upon themselves to lower discount rates below market rates to "stimulate" the economy, then to raise them above market rates to prevent gold losses, losses that would not have occurred had the original "stimulus" not been attempted.

Central banking accompanied increased government intervention in hitherto private economic matters. Eichengreen (1992) observes how "issues that had previously remained outside the political sphere, such as the determination of the level of wages and employment, suddenly became politicized" and how, as a result "doubt was cast over the credibility of the commitment [to gold convertibility]. No longer did capital necessarily flow in stabilizing directions.... The decisions of central bankers, long regarded as obscure, became grist for the political mill.... Unable to balance government budgets, politicians enlisted the central bank's monetary printing presses to finance their deficits ... resulting in episodes of inflationary chaos and economic turmoil ..."(9). In better days, "convertibility provided a visible signal that a government's financial house was in order, and the gold standard inspired confidence on the part of domestic savers and foreign investors." But after the war, "in an effort to maintain confidence, governments sought to disguise the extent of currency depreciation. They maintained convertibility *de jure* even when suspending it *de facto*"(230). Thus, central banks financed expansionist governments and interfered with the gold standard by following a contradictory policy of "maintaining confidence" by cheating.

Similar contradictions abound in Eichengreen's account of the Federal Reserve System and its treatment of gold. He asserts that "one rationale for creating the Federal Reserve System in December 1913 was to manage the American gold standard more effectively" (1992, p. 31). Indeed, the Fed's original charter mandated that its currency be convertible into gold, but this provision was more a reflection of the classical gold standard that was passing into history than it was an accurate indication of how a central bank might manage gold in the future. In fact, "the arrival of the Fed on the international scene was a significant departure from the prewar era," for "the new institution was unpredictable" and "the establishment of a central bank with discretionary powers contributed to the politicization of monetary policymaking in the U.S." (1992, pp. 9, 12). He concedes that "what was inadequately appreciated was that by creating a central bank ... the U.S. government might exacerbate the cyclical instability of the domestic economy" (64).

What can be concluded from such a record? Surely *unpredictability*, *politicization*, *inflating*, and *cheating* cannot be interpreted as being compatible with the smooth operation of a gold standard. Far from being the "guardians" of the gold standard, central banks have been the proverbial foxes guarding the hen houses. R. S. Sayers, an advocate of central banking, explains why the gold standard cannot be its primary concern:

> The essence of central banking is discretionary control of the monetary system.... Under some circumstances the purpose of central banking might be defined as the maintenance of the gold standard, the maintenance of a sterling standard, or the maintenance of a dollar standard. But these varieties are of purpose; central banking is an institutional arrangement that may be made to serve any one of a number of purposes.... [But] working to rule is the antithesis of central banking. A central bank is necessary only when the community decides that a discretionary element is desirable. The central banker is the man who exercises this discretion, not the machine that works according to rule. (Sayers, 1957, p. 1.)

The gold standard is an objective restraint, and therefore the complete opposite of central banking, which is arbitrary. But Sayers argues that money itself is arbitrary and therefore legitimately can be managed by government. As he puts it, "if there were any basic money the supply of which at all times determined according to fixed rules the behavior of every conceivable financial institution, there would be no logical point in governing the supply of that money according to fixed rules. But there is not ..." There is no agreement on what constitutes money, he says, "for the very good reason that any definition is necessarily arbitrary" (1957, pp. 5-6). Sayers concludes:

> It is idle to say that one can somewhere find an ultimate form of money and rule that off as the grand regulator of the economic situation, a regulator that can be made to behave properly by legislator's orders. Our economic systems are not like that. So we must have central bankers to exercise a discretionary influence upon the monetary situation. And it follows that there is no eternal code of rules for them to follow. (Sayers, 1957, pp. 6-7.)

The theory of central banking rests on arbitrariness and politics, not economics or the objective value of gold. The clash between statism and gold also is apparent when viewed in historical perspective. Gold and gold-convertible paper evolved as the market's choice of superior money. Central banking evolved as a means of financing deficit-ridden governments. Gold money developed as an objective value managed by rational rules for the benefit of profit-seeking private banks and their customers. Fiat paper money developed as a subjective value, managed by the arbitrary discretion of central bankers for the benefit of revenue-seeking governments. The gold standard rose up under the rule of law and flourished in the age of laissez-faire capitalism (the 19th century). Central banking rose up under the rule of men and flourished in the age of central planning and statism (the 20th century).

These basic distinctions — between free banking and the gold standard, on the one hand, and central banking and fiat paper money, on the other — explain why activist central banking and the gold standard are inimical and historically have never coincided for very long. In the century leading up to World War I, the gold standard was operated by relatively free banks and by relatively powerless central banks that had not yet monopolized money. Between World War I and the Great Depression, central banks were granted full monopolies on currency and began removing gold from the private banking system. At first, central banks kept their currencies convertible into gold. However, ever since the Great Depression, apart from a brief decade when the Bretton Woods system was fully operative (1958-68), central banks have issued inconvertible fiat paper currency. This evolution from privately managed gold to government managed paper was necessitated by the growth of government and especially of the welfare state. In short, money was politicized.

Those who actively opposed the gold standard in the 1930s tended to blame free markets for the Great Depression. They also recognized the

91

connection between the growth of big government and the need to abandon gold. According to Alan Greenspan:

> The opposition to the gold standard in any form — from a growing number of welfare-state advocates — was prompted by a much subtler insight; the realization that the gold standard is incompatible with chronic deficit spending (the hallmark of the welfare state). Stripped of its academic jargon, the welfare state is nothing more than a mechanism by which governments confiscate the wealth of the productive members of a society to support a wide variety of welfare schemes. A substantial part of the confiscation is effected by taxation. But the welfare statists were quick to recognize that if they wished to retain political power, the amount of taxation had to be limited and they had to resort to programs of massive deficit spending, *i.e.*, they had to borrow money, by issuing government bonds, to finance welfare expenditures on a large scale.... But government bonds are not backed by tangible wealth, only by the government's promise to pay out of future tax revenues, and cannot be easily absorbed by the financial markets.... Government deficit spending under a gold standard is severely limited. The abandonment of the gold standard made it possible for the welfare statists to use the banking system as a means to an unlimited expansion of credit. They have created paper reserves in the form of government bonds which — through a complex series of steps — the banks accept in place of tangible assets and treat as if they were an actual deposit, *i.e.*, as the equivalent of what was formerly a deposit of gold. The law of supply and demand is not to be conned. As the supply of money (of claims) increases relative to the supply of tangible assets in the economy, prices must eventually rise.... In the absence of a gold standard, there is no way to protect savings from confiscation through inflation. There is no safe store of value. If there were, the government would have to make its holding illegal, as was done in the case of gold.... Deficit spending is simply a scheme for the hidden confiscation of wealth. Gold stands in the way of this insidious process. It stands as a protector of property rights. (Greenspan, 1967.)

We know that one prominent advocate of the welfare state, Paul Samuelson, has vigorously defended central banking while opposing free banking. Elsewhere he has argued that "any attempt to legitimize an historically extinct whig laissez-faire ... represents Humpty-Dumptyism." In other words, echoing Karl Marx, Samuelson believes the advance of statism is inexorable. His self-admitted philosophy is sympathetic to the real redistributive purposes of central banking when he derides as a myth that there are "sacred property rights," and insists that "redistributive welfare transfers are not coercions on people by an external state ..." (Szenberg, 1992, p. 9). Just as there is a "philosophy of the gold standard" that supports it and makes it flourish, there is a philosophy of central banking and fiat

92

money that makes it possible. Samuelson expresses this latter philosophy, the one prevailing in this century, quite consistently.

The Destructiveness of Inflating and Deflating

Fluctuations in the value of money are disruptive to economic stability and prosperity. Fluctuating money brings fluctuations in prices, including interest rates — the price of credit. In turn, fluctuating prices contribute to confusion, miscalculation, and discoordination in the marketplace. While it is true that prices fluctuate continually in a free market, this reflects real underlying changes in supply and demand conditions for particular goods and services. When prices fluctuate in a context of unsound money, however, the markets receive mixed signals. There is no easy way of distinguishing whether price changes reflect changes in supply and demand or changes in the value of money itself. Worse, changes in the value of money do not affect all markets simultaneously or similarly. Markets that are otherwise coordinated become discoordinated (von Mises, 1978).

Attempts to treat the symptoms of inflating or deflating with price controls or price supports only add to the distortions by causing shortages or surpluses. Inflating is especially pernicious in the way it corrodes the value of financial assets held as savings. When higher price inflation is unanticipated, and often it is given the arbitrary manner in which it is imposed, creditors are harmed at the expense of debtors. Given the fact that in this century profligate governments have become the world's largest debtors, a policy of inflating is a policy of destructive confiscation. Deflations, although rarer, are no less disruptive and also are characteristic of fiat paper money. It is little wonder that producers and savers tend to flee from countries that adopt such policies and head for safer havens elsewhere in the world.

History shows that fluctuations in the value of money are narrowly contained under a gold coin standard, while they are greatest under fiat paper systems operated by central banks (Paarlberg, 1993). Nevertheless, the alleged ability of central bankers to curtail speculative episodes and their aftermaths, remains a staple argument of the proponents of central banking. However, there is a significant difference between the follies of bankers and investors under sound money and under fiat money. As Arthur Okun observed:

> The opportunity of safe saving is lost in a period of sizable and unpredictable price increases. Some assets offer a degree of protection against inflation in the sense that their values are likely to move up as consumer prices rise. But no asset shows a good year-by-year correlation with prices; even corporate equities and real estate are not good anti-inflationary hedges by this test. They may actually tend to outpace the price level

on the average in the long run, but only with wide swings and great uncertainty.

Our financial system ought to serve both investors who want to earn maximum returns (and are willing to take substantial risks) and holders of reasonably safe assets who view their saving largely as deferred consumption. The latter are not accommodated during inflation … [and] the unsophisticated saver who is merely preparing for the proverbial rainy day becomes a sucker. (Okun, 1970, p. 20.)

In short, under fiat money, everyone must speculate (often on the basis of rumors and hunches about the future actions of the central bankers). Under a gold standard, one can concentrate on production. Even if one believes the doubtful proposition that fluctuations and credit cycles under the gold standard were in some sense worse than those under fiat money, it is incontestable that those who suffered most before central banking were those who chose to speculate. Today, the holding of fiat currency is itself a speculation.

The world's wealth grew most under free banking and the gold standard and as a consequence of its prevailing context of free markets and private property. Despite higher living standards today, the rate of economic growth has slowed considerably under central banking and fiat paper money. Central banking has generated an unstable monetary climate damaging to growth and prosperity. The world's wealth today would have been much greater in the absence of central banking. Whatever degree of wealth exists in the world today was achieved *in spite of* central banking and its monetary manipulations, not because of it.

The Keynesian school of economics has opposed the gold standard and advocated inflating more than any other school in this century. Yet John Maynard Keynes, at one time an active member of the Fabian Society (which promoted socialism) in London, knew full well the detrimental effects of inflating on free markets, and echoed the insights of the father of Russian Communism:

Lenin is said to have declared that the best way to destroy the Capitalist System was to debauch the currency. By a continuing process of inflation, governments can confiscate, secretly and unobserved, an important part of the wealth of their citizens. By this method they not only confiscate, but they confiscate *arbitrarily*; and, while the process impoverishes many, it actually enriches some. The sight of this arbitrary rearrangement of riches strikes not only at the security but at the confidence in the equity of the existing distribution of wealth. Those to whom the system brings windfalls beyond their deserts and even beyond their expectations or desires, become 'profiteers,' who are the object of the hatred of the bourgeoisie, whom the inflationism has impoverished, not less than the proletariat. As the inflation proceeds, and the real value of the currency fluctuates wildly from month to month, all permanent relations between debtors and creditors, which form the ultimate foundation of capitalism, become so utterly disordered as to be almost meaningless; and the process of wealth-getting degenerates into a gamble and a lottery. Lenin was certainly right. There is no subtler, no surer means of overthrowing the existing basis of society than to debauch the currency. The process engages all the hidden forces of economic law on the side of destruction, and it does it in a manner which not one man in a million is able to diagnose. (Keynes, 1920, p. 235-236.)

This insightful passage by Keynes, one of the best accounts of inflating's true harm, is all the more remarkable given that Keynes and his followers so readily endorsed inflating. Keynes did so in part because he endorsed socialism. However, there is a further, deeper insight to be added to his own assessment, namely, that there is no subtler, no surer means of debauching any currency than to establish central banking. Another socialist and contemporary of Keynes, playwright George Bernard Shaw, recognized the crucial difference between gold money and government money, better than most economists today:

To sum up, the most important thing about money is to maintain its stability, so that a pound will buy as much a year hence or ten years hence or fifty years hence as today, and no more. With paper money, this stability has to be maintained by the Government. With a gold currency it tends to maintain itself even when the natural supply of gold is increased by discoveries of new deposits, because of the curious fact that demand for gold in the world is practically infinite. You have to choose (as a voter) between trusting to the natural stability of gold and the natural stability of the Government. And, with due respect for these gentlemen, I advise you, as long as the Capitalist system lasts, to vote for gold. (Shaw, 1928, p. 263.)

Sadly, in this century, it has been the enemies of freedom and capitalism who seem to have understood best what gold represents. Their insights show that statist politics, not bad economics, undermined gold.

Modern Defenders of Central Banking

Economists who recognize that central banking is not justified on economic grounds nevertheless defend its power to inflate and generate revenues for government. They publish articles about "the optimal rate of inflation," that is, the rate central banks might impose to "surprise" the markets, prevent countervailing "escape" tactics, and generate the most revenue for government. These articles are equivalent to telling burglars how best to rob homes or advising terrorists how best to create explosives.

This is what passes for monetary analysis today. The confiscatory aspect of inflating is fully understood, recognized, accepted, and then examined in terms of "optimization." This attitude could not be more removed from honesty, justice, and integrity — the philosophy of the gold standard.

A growing number of today's younger economists, more respectful of freedom, embrace free banking and the gold standard. But the majority of older economists, many trained in the aftermath of the Great Depression, still support central banking and fiat paper money. Some of their students carry on the belief in government money as well. As mentioned, many do so purely on statist grounds. They simply want big government and are unwilling to jettison its primary banker. Paul Samuelson and the Keynesians are in this camp. Their alleged opponents, Milton Friedman and the monetarists, tend to defend government money on economic grounds. They argue that a monetary system left to its own devices is inherently unstable. To that extent, they argue, free market money makes the economy unstable. Thus, it is argued, central banking is needed to stabilize money, banking, and the economy. Elsewhere, Friedman argues as a classical liberal, but in his one area of specialty, money, he is an interventionist.

The monetarists are no less a friend of central banking or an enemy of the gold standard than the Keynesians, although for slightly different reasons. The Keynesians dismiss gold as a "barbarous relic" even though it was the foundation for the most modern and integrated system of international money ever achieved. The monetarists dismiss gold as "just another commodity" even though it is the most remarkable of all time, the one commodity men converged on as money, and have accumulated over the centuries. Both agree that gold is costly to produce. The Keynesians ridicule the process by which gold is dug out of the ground from one part of the earth and buried in vaults elsewhere, ignoring the fact that is was central banks, not free markets, that placed gold off limits in this way. Monetarists decry the "resource costs" undertaken to produce, transfer, and store gold and stress that paper is cheaper to produce, ignoring the fact that this is one of gold's great virtues, and well worth the price paid voluntarily by markets. Elsewhere, monetarists seem able to trust markets to decide.

Other superficial differences exist. Keynesians want central banks to have complete and unlimited discretion to do whatever they or their sponsoring governments wish. Monetarists want central banks to behave responsibly, to rule according to rules. Both camps are unified in their defense of central banking and their opposition to the gold standard. Both envision central bankers as philosopher-kings, able to see things mere mortals cannot, able to correct problems that free markets allegedly generate. The common ground on which these allegedly uncommon schools stand is further evidence of the incompatibility of central banking and gold. The errors of both the Keynesians and monetarists is perhaps best captured in this criticism by Sayers of arguments against central banking:

> Most of these arguments [in favor of gold] boil down to an assertion that men are not to be trusted with discretionary powers, and that departures from automatism in the regulation of the monetary system may sooner or later lead to trouble ... It is not difficult to support this attitude by reference to the monetary history of any country.... [But] people have not always blundered thoughtlessly or immorally; it is rather that there are traps in the very nature of monetary policy. There is, for instance, the inherent difficulty of making the right decision sufficiently early ... [and] when the central banker has to choose between two courses, one of which is politically disagreeable, he is strongly tempted to doubt the diagnosis that urges the disagreeable course.... The difficulty of early diagnosis coupled with ordinary human weakness thus gives to central banking an inflationary bias.... Discretionary control of the monetary system bears within itself the risks of exaggerating the ups and downs of trade and of undermining the value of the monetary unit. Yet the elimination of the trade cycle and the conservation of the value of money are among the most important aims of monetary policy.... Central bankers may become more conscious of their responsibilities ... and may infect business men themselves with something of their coldness.... *The central banker must be superhuman....* [But] these inherent weaknesses in central banking can, at any rate in most countries, be kept within manageable bounds.... As experience in central banking accumulates, it is reasonable to expect that the inherent weaknesses will be kept increasingly under control.... The strength of these arguments in support of central banking is necessarily a matter of opinion. Those who are more afraid of human weakness and less confident in man's capacity to master his economic environment may logically enough protest that the case for central banking is not strong enough. (Sayers, 1957, p. 3-5, emphasis added.)

Sayers concedes that historically, central banking has led to trouble, that it fosters business cycles and undermines the value of money, that there are real problems and "inherent weaknesses" in the central planning of money, and that central bankers must be omniscient and "superhuman." Both Keynesians and monetarists would agree with this grim assessment, but at the same time would agree that central banking must proceed unhindered. Central banking, they argue, must be made more "manageable." Central bankers must try harder and must be permitted to learn on the job. This is preposterous. If free banking and the gold standard had ever delivered such poor results, they would have been denounced and abandoned long ago. Ironically, they *were*, although their performance was superior.

Opposition to central banking does not depend on some belief in human "weakness" or in some inevitable tendency toward dishonesty or ignorance in economic decision making, as Sayers suggests. That approach says central planning would be fine if only the right men were chosen to wield its levers of power. Is the Federal Reserve System any less arbitrary for having Alan Greenspan, a former advocate of the gold standard and free banking, as its head? Not in the least. The current occupants of central bank board seats cannot change the political incentives those seats entail. Those occupants are far more likely to become politicians during their tenure, if they are not politically oriented before they arrive, than they are likely to transform those seats into chairs of independent scholarship.

The notion that central banks are engaged in objective, politics-free, scientific endeavors is sheer fantasy. Nevertheless, it is the main working premise of establishment economists and financial journalists. The fantasy nevertheless perpetuates a never-ending search for the "right" government planner. This is a great danger, because the problem is government planning itself. Government planning means the imposition of legal restrictions and edicts — of force, pure and simple — in matters that should be left to voluntary private markets. Free markets — in money as in any other field — do not rest on a view of mankind in general as depraved and particular men as unfit to plan. The argument for free markets recognizes that force is inimical to rational judgment, free enterprise, and sound money. Rational planning and the incentives that drive it exist only in the private sector. Free markets reflect confidence that men can make sound uncoerced decisions without the interference of bureaucrats and politicians.

What explains the continued embrace of central banking in the face of such poor performance? Politics, not economics. The Keynesians want big government. The monetarists seem to want smaller government, but not in the field of money. Milton Friedman has observed with irony that the Federal Reserve simultaneously has the worst track record of any U.S. Government agency and also the highest reputation. Yet he has contributed more than any other economist to this result by continuing to advise the Fed on how to behave better — an approach that assumes the Fed has both the interest and capacity to do so. Friedman and other monetarists also have opposed the reintroduction of the gold standard on the grounds that it would not be politically feasible. Obviously, this argument has nothing to do with economics. It means only that monetarists are no better equipped than Keynesians to supply the intellectual-legal-political arguments needed to defend gold.

There are other, increasingly prominent schools of economics that oppose both the Keynesians and monetarists on a number of issues, and on money in particular. Both the "supply-siders," represented by Robert Mundell of Columbia University, and the "new classical" school, represented by Robert Barro of Harvard, generally defend gold money and the gold standard, while doubting the capacity or willingness of central banks to perform well. The roots of both schools are in classical economics, in the writings of Adam Smith, David Ricardo, and John Stuart Mill, all of whom were defenders of free banking and the gold standard. However, unlike their predecessors, the supply-siders and the new classicals tend to believe central banks can be made to manage a gold standard.

Some supply-siders have endorsed the idea of a "price rule," whereby central banks conduct monetary policy by targeting a narrowly fluctuating price of gold. This is in slight contrast to the monetarists, who ask central banks to conduct monetary policy by a "quantity" (of money) rule. The new classical economists also defend the gold standard on the ground that it can instill central banking with a credible commitment to rule. Both supply-siders and new classicals tend to view the gold standard as a worthy model of monetary integrity, but tend not to recognize the true purpose of central banking and how it undermined that standard.

The modern Austrian economists, represented by Lawrence White, defend both fractional-reserve free banking and the classical gold standard, as did the founder of the school, Carl Menger (1840-1921), and its most prominent 20th century defender, Ludwig von Mises (1881-1973). Other Austrians, however, have advocated free banking without gold money (Friedrich Hayek) or gold money without free banking (Murray Rothbard). Thus, even in schools that respect gold money, it is only rarely recognized that gold must be accompanied by free banking, and in schools that respect free banking, that it requires a gold anchor.

Some economists who recognize the damage done by central banking and glimpse its political genesis have begun to study and urge central bank "independence" (Alesina and Summers, 1993). In other words, there are attempts to salvage the reputation and future of central banks by ensuring that they are somehow made independent of government. This is not possible, however, given the central purpose of central banking. Nevertheless, the sudden scramble to impart credibility and independence to central banks may lead to a beneficial outcome. The logical end of this search is the complete privatization or abolition of central banks. No bank is more free of government control than a truly "free bank" under a gold standard.

Central banking survives today because it is widely supported by advocates of central planning as a utopian ideal. One particularly fawning writer refers to central banks as "Platonic guardians" and "disinterested protectors of the public good," despite the "dismal experience of monetary policy under the management of politicians" (Plender, 1994). A staunch critic of this premise, economist Edward Kane, has observed in the instance of the Federal Reserve System, that:

[Economists] typically treat the Federal Reserve System as a sovereign decision maker, whose managers seek singlemindedly to promote the public interest at every turn. From this perspective, choosing strategy and tactics for monetary control becomes a straightforward exercise in applied welfare economics ... Inherent in the utopian view of the Fed is the presumption that the Fed can somehow evaluate the public interest on its own.... This utopian conception of Fed intentions and tactics is carefully nurtured in Fed publications and official statements. Fed leaders depict themselves as waiting in anguish for the economics profession finally to develop an adequate model of how monetary policy truly works. By this subtle open-mouth policy, Fed officials distribute guilt from poor policy performance to economists and shape the way that the Fed is portrayed in money-and-banking textbooks and in most professional research.... [But] the Fed is a political institution designed *by* politicians to *serve* politicians.... The Fed acts first and foremost as a political animal. (Kane, 1980.)

Kane captures the generally naive interpretation granted to the Fed by most economists. This is the model of Plato's "philosopher king." As long as central banking is considered an ideal, or utopia, it will live on and continue its destructive ways. As long as the "public interest" is discussed as a legitimate concept, or as anything other than what it is, namely, the specific interests of government officials, central banking will persist. When central banking and fiat money are seen for what they really are, and free banking and the gold standard are seen again as ideal, a better system will evolve.

Why do central banks continue to hold gold reserves, long after they defaulted on gold and issued inconvertible paper money? According to a senior official of the Bank of Italy, "we think it is important given the overall economic situation in Italy, to keep our gold reserves. Gold is psychologically considered to be important as an instrument to back the currency, given the indebtedness of the state" (*The Wall Street Journal*, 1993). The U.S. Gold Commission made similar observations in 1982 when it considered activating Federal Reserve gold reserves. What does it mean? That government debt securities lose their value with every new wave of inflation, and always run the risk of a complete loss in value, whereas gold never loses its value. Gold is the "final asset" that is no one's obligation. A central bank's value and credibility have more to do with the gold it holds than anything else.

In both theory and history, central banking is inimical to gold money. As evidence in Chapter II makes clear, free banking — the unregulated, competitive issuance of gold-convertible money — is the most appropriate banking system for a free economy. If the world ever returns to gold, it will have to throw off the scourge of central banking — and the welfare state it aims to finance — in the process.

VIII.

GOLD AS A BAROMETER AND INVESTMENT

THE price of gold is quoted in most financial news updates, together with the Dow Jones Industrials Average (DJIA) and the foreign exchange value of the dollar. But few people can say *why* gold is given such attention, given that it has long since been removed from the monetary system. Recognized or not, the price of gold is one of the most important and accurate barometers of financial trends available to an investor. The price of gold itself can be used as a predictor of monetary trends and hence financial asset returns. The future price of gold is relevant to investors in gold. Can the gold price be predicted? If so, by which factors? What principles should guide investments in gold?

The Gold Price: A Barometer of Paper Money Values

Since the abandonment of gold money by governments in August 1971, gold prices denominated in every government currency have fluctuated dramatically. Since then the price of gold in terms of currency has increased markedly. Attempts have been made to fix or "manage" the exchange rates among paper currencies, but not between paper currencies and gold. In the United States, the dollar price of gold has risen from $35 per ounce in 1971 to about $850 per ounce in 1980, before falling below $300 per ounce in 1985, rising to $450 per ounce in 1986, falling to $330 per ounce in February 1993 and rising above $400 per ounce 7 months later. The price of gold has fluctuated even more in terms of most other currencies in the world, but less in terms of the few currencies that have been "stronger" than the dollar, such as the Japanese yen, Deutsche mark, or Swiss franc. What accounts for these gyrations?

Consider the dollar price of gold. Since the unit of account in the United States is the dollar and all goods and services necessarily are denominated in that currency, changes in the prices of dollar-denominated items usually are interpreted as reflecting the supply and demand factors of that commodity, not the value of the dollar itself. For example, if the price of corn oscillates severely, most likely it has something to do with bumper crops, or crop failures, or the weather. If the price of computer chips tumbles, probably it has something to do with technological advances in the production of chips. As with other commodities, it sometimes is believed that when the gold price fluctuates, it must reflect instability. Many gold analysts routinely scrutinize mining trends as well as the identified activities of buyers and sellers of gold to predict its price, or else they dismiss the price as driven by fickle investors clinging to a barbarous relic.

But gold is no ordinary commodity and it defies ordinary supply-demand analyses. As history shows, gold is money, regardless of its prevailing legal treatment. Moreover, gold is the only money that has been accepted and adopted by people worldwide. Gold means the same thing to everyone who values it, regardless of the government they live under. Unlike every other commodity, gold is simultaneously imperishable, liquid and uniform. Gold is never lacking for buyers. Most important for interpreting the meaning of its price, as discussed above, is that gold is produced for *accumulation*, not consumption. Gold's primary function is as a liquid store of wealth, not as an industrial input or item of consumption.

Unlike gold, the annual output of consumed commodities dwarfs aboveground supplies and changes in supply can severely alter real prices. Floods can destroy crops and boost agricultural prices. In its heyday, OPEC could restrict annual oil output and do the same to oil prices. Gold is different. Virtually all the gold that has ever been mined throughout history still exists today in aboveground stocks. Gold is rarely lost, because of its high value. According to the World Gold Council and Gold Fields Mineral Services Ltd., the known world gold stock today is about 3.5 billion ounces. The annual output of the world's gold mines — today about 70 million ounces — is about 2 percent of the total stock. Even when large gold discoveries were made — in Latin America in the 16th century, in California in the decade after 1848, and in the Yukon, South America, and Australia starting in the 1890s — the world supply of gold increased by only small increments each year. Annual additions to the aboveground gold stock alone simply are too small to account for marked changes in the price of gold. The relevant gold supply is not the production of gold from the mines every year but the total stock of gold that has been accumulated. Nor is the buying and selling of gold a main determinant of changes in the gold price. Even today's large gold transactions are but a drop in the ocean of the world stock of gold.

The fact that gold is accumulated, not consumed, means that the purchasing power of gold — what it will buy in terms of other goods and services — varies within a relatively narrow range over long periods. Extensive empirical evidence collected by Jastram (1977) confirms this general point. Gold exhibits a relatively constant purchasing power. It should continue to do so.

Mechanics of the London "Fix"

Gold is traded in many forms and places throughout the world. In the teeming bazaars and *souks* of the eastern hemisphere, relatively crude and heavy jewelry or the ancient *tael* bars may be the center of attention. In the "pits" of the commodity exchanges, traders use frenzied signals to buy and sell contracts to deliver gold at some future date. Almost anywhere in the world, bankers and coin dealers calmly trade gold "bullion" coins or bars of gold with their customers.

Yet, twice a day, they all pause in their labors to get word of the London "fix," so they can adjust their offers and bids to world conditions. This takes place in London in the mid-morning (the a.m. fix) and in the mid-afternoon (the p.m. fix). At these sessions, the representatives of several British bullion dealers take their places around a table. Each sits behind a small Union Jack, with a telephone connected to his office by his side.

The host begins the proceedings by announcing a price. Dealers who are willing to buy at that price tip their flags down, and those who are willing to sell leave them up. If all the flags are up, then a lower price will be announced, and if all the flags are down, a higher price will be tested. Conversation is restricted to hushed and hurried telephone consultations with each firm's headquarters. When a price is found that leaves some flags up and some down, each participant indicates how much he is willing to buy or sell. The chairman will then suggest ways to dispose of any discrepancies, so that all the gold to be traded at that session will have the same price.

Only then will the "fix" be announced to outsiders. The dealers never state the amount they traded nor do they indicate whether they traded for clients or their own accounts. It is even possible that no gold at all changes hands in a given session. Nevertheless, the word of the "fix" is flashed around the world in a few moments, and even where it is the middle of the night, say, in Hong Kong, San Francisco, or Dubai, someone is up and waiting for the news.

The London "fix" appears to reflect the decision of just a few individuals, but in fact it is the only truly global gold market. This mechanism links all the markets in the world together and is the single most reliable indicator of the worldwide price of gold. Contrary to popular belief, the gold price is not susceptible to manipulation by a handful of dealers.

What does the price of gold reflect? Since the real value of gold is roughly constant over time, changes in the gold price in any given currency reflect changes in the market's estimate of the value of that currency. In effect, the gold price is the inverse of the price of paper money. A rising price of gold reflects inflationary forces while a falling price of gold reflects disinflationary forces. The quoted price of gold is the price of fiat currency in terms of genuine money. Since gold is money that cannot be debased, it tends to measure paper money debasement best. Gold demand reflects investors' fluctuating confidence in paper money. Thus gyrations in the dollar price of gold should not be interpreted to mean that gold is a fickle commodity buffeted by the whims of "gold bugs." When the price of gold varies, it is the value of the paper currency, not of gold itself, that is varying most.

The fact that the price of gold is the inverse of the price of paper money helps interpret recent financial history. Thus it is not coincidental that the tenfold rise in the dollar price of gold since President Roosevelt devalued the dollar to 1/35 of an ounce of gold has been associated with a similar rise in the dollar prices of other tangible items, such as cars, homes, appliances, food, and clothing. An ounce of gold still buys roughly the same "quantity of car" as it did 60 years ago. But that is not the situation for the paper dollar. Nor is it coincidental that the rise in the dollar price of gold to about $850 per ounce in 1980 accompanied a worldwide "dollar crisis," and widespread distrust of U.S. policies. The subsequent decline of the gold price to below $400 per ounce during the latter half of 1980s reflected a restoration of confidence in U.S. policies under President Reagan.

A few lessons may be learned from gold price swings in the dollar gold price during the 1980s. First, a rise in the gold price — that is, a loss of confidence in the dollar — is neither inexorable nor irreversible. A mere extrapolation of recent trends is never justified. Second, central banks may adopt less reckless policies in order to avoid major reforms that might threaten their power. When the U.S. Gold Commission convened in 1981-82 to discuss ways to restore discipline to the monetary system, it got the attention of many central bankers who opposed such a move. Opponents of gold made sure that Federal Reserve Board members were on the Commission. Gold was rejected as an option, but Federal Reserve policy became far less inflationary thereafter. Third, confidence in the dollar can be restored to some degree despite very high budget deficits. Deficits themselves are not inflationary. Only if they are financed by central bank monetization do they contribute to inflationary pressures. Although the U.S. national debt quadrupled in the 1980s, there was not the inordinate degree of central bank monetization that would have brought significantly higher price inflation (Salsman, 1993).

The fact that gold prices primarily are a measure of paper money values tells investors a lot about the expected performance of financial assets, such as stocks and bonds, that are denominated in such currencies (see Ranson, 1990 and 1992; Salsman, 1994). A higher price of gold in any currency is an indicator of higher price inflation, a context in which financial assets do poorly compared to tangibles. On the other hand, a declining price of gold is a harbinger of disinflation, when financial assets often do well compared to tangibles.

The gold price also may be a forecaster of interest rates, which themselves reflect not only credit risk, but price inflation risk. All else equal, interest rates will be higher under price inflation, as lenders seek compensation for being repaid in cheaper money. Interest rates, in turn, heavily influence the business cycle and investment returns on common stocks.

Higher gold prices portend higher interest rates, which ultimately are bearish for the economy, corporate profits, and equities. Lower gold prices and lower interest rates are bullish for the economy and equities. The gold price also is a good forecaster of bonds; when the gold price rises (falls), bond prices usually fall (rise) in the following year.

Finally, gold is a good device for distinguishing the relative strength of currencies. In an age of floating exchange rates, it is difficult to determine which currencies are strong or weak without first converting them into gold, an independent reference point of real money. For example, the U.S. dollar fell nearly 30 percent against the Japanese yen in the early years of both the Carter and Clinton administrations. Why, then, have price inflation and interest rates not risen as high under Clinton as they did under Carter? The dollar price of gold has risen about 17 percent under Clinton (to date), whereas it rose more than 100 percent over the same period under Carter. The latest decline in the dollar versus the yen is partly explained by dollar inflation, but to a great extent also by yen deflation (reflected in a *falling* yen price of gold).

Gold tends to perform better than other commodities as a forecaster of underlying price trends, because it is the one liquid commodity that is accumulated instead of consumed. Price inflation is a fall in the purchasing power of money that is reflected in the *general* level of prices. Price increases in particular markets may reflect conditions unique to that market. The *relative* prices of commodities such as oil or raw industrial materials change with the business cycle and exogenous events. Gold, however, is not a major input to industry. Changes in the gold price are thus the purest barometer of changes in currency values — in the *absolute* level of prices. Whether the price of gold is rising or falling, whether or not central banks pay any attention to it, gold is always measuring paper money. Whether or not governments have allowed markets to use gold as a medium of exchange, gold has always served as a standard of value. Thus gold can measure the fluctuating value of paper currencies.

What then determines the price of gold? Some popular candidates may be discounted at the outset. The price of gold is not determined primarily by supply conditions within the gold industry itself, nor by gold's cost of production. Supply does not change enough to matter. Nor is the gold price driven by particular buy-sell transactions between speculators, central banks, or commodity funds that are reported periodically in the financial press. As we have seen, these are too small to matter. Nor is jewelry demand a major factor. The money supply and the national debt are other factors believed to influence gold. Both aggregates have grown significantly in the United States over the past dozen years, precisely when the dollar price of gold fell by half. What about wars? These do not necessarily drive the gold price;

the dollar gold price did not move much at all in response to the Gulf War in 1990-91.

The overriding factor determining the gold price in any currency is the degree of credibility exhibited (or likely to be exhibited) by the government that issues the currency. The higher (lower) the credibility, the more (less) likely a government currency will retain its value or not lose (gain) so much, and the more (less) likely the gold price denominated in that currency will stabilize or fall (rise). Since there no longer are any objective standards by which government money is issued, no precise formula exists for determining the long-term future value of a currency, and therefore the future of its gold price. All government currencies tend to decline in value over time, although at variable rates. There is an inflationary bias built into central banking and fiat paper money. But government policies that are generally *unfavorable* to markets — such as higher tax rates, more regulation, protectionism, devaluations, and capital controls — tend to undermine government credibility and raise the rate of price inflation the most. Debt monetization by central banks also undermines credibility. Budget deficits are a necessary, but not a sufficient, condition for such monetization, but all else equal, deficit spending makes debasement more likely and undermines government credibility.

Government policies unfavorable to markets have been enacted in the United States through most of this century, but especially under the administrations of Roosevelt (1932-45), Nixon (1968-74) and Carter (1977-80). Not coincidentally, these were the administrations that either rejected gold money or, having abandoned it, presided over large increases in the gold price. Policies that are generally *favorable* toward markets bolster the credibility of government and lend confidence to its currency. In the post-World War II era in the United States, the administrations of Eisenhower (1953-60) and Reagan (1981-88) were the most pro-market. Gold prices were stable or falling in these years, and financial markets soared.

Historically, anti-market policies have been most pronounced outside the United States, especially in Latin America and Eastern Europe. These regions have experienced the worst price inflation rates and the most rapidly rising gold prices, denominated in local currency. In some instances, governments may take specific steps to bolster credibility. In 1991 for example, Argentina enacted a law that limits the issuance of local currency in direct correspondence to the issuing agency's reserves of U.S. dollars and gold. Argentina brought its hyperinflation down to single digit rates overnight. Such discipline, however, must be part of a wider commitment to protect private property and abide by the rule of law. In situations where this is not occurring, as in Russia, no amount of currency reform, even using gold, can succeed. The credibility is lacking. Short of observing such specifically defined rules, there is no clear way of gauging whether a statist government will maintain the value of its currency. But whatever it does, the gold price of that currency will gauge it accurately.

Gold as an Investment: Coin, Bullion, and Mining Shares

Those who still insist that gold is a barbarous relic of the past must wonder why there remains so much interest in gold as an investment even today. People still mine gold, transport it, store it, insure it, and consider it precious, as they did centuries ago. The explanation is not that gold investors are inherently irrational or mystical. The reason for continued interest in gold lies in the fact that it retains its historical attributes of liquidity, stability, and universal acceptance, despite the attacks on it by envious governments. No government paper money has ever delivered the benefits of gold.

For more than 4 decades (March 1933 until December 1974) it was illegal for American citizens to own gold. During the 2 decades since ownership was legalized, Americans have been accumulating gold as an investment. At first Americans bought foreign-made gold coins, such as the South African Kruggerand. In 1986, the U.S. Treasury began reissuing gold Eagle coins for the first time since 1933, this time as an investment, not as money. The source of gold for these new coins was the gold originally taken from the American people. The U.S. Government now sells the gold it once confiscated.

Why is gold held today as an investment, but not used as a medium of exchange? Because the legal tender laws remain in place. These laws require that market participants accept the U.S. paper dollar (and other national currencies) in transactions. When the U.S. Treasury began issuing gold coins again in 1986, the one-ounce coins were marked with the inscription "fifty dollars," even though the actual market value was ten times higher. Since a "dollar" today means the legal tender paper money issued by the U.S. Government, inscribing "fifty dollars" on gold coins guaranteed they would not circulate as money. No one will pay for anything with an ounce of gold that American courts will say is worth only a fraction of its real value. This policy is an indication of how much the Government itself recognizes the superiority of gold money. Why did the U.S. Government begin reissuing gold coins in 1986? A handful of U.S. Congressmen pushed for the change after the U.S. Gold Commission (1982) rejected a return to the gold standard. Subsequently, gold was legalized.

Although the investment characteristics of gold coin, gold bullion, and gold mining shares differ, each of these asset classes is sensitive to the same factors that influence the gold price. In addition, investors should be aware that premiums, commissions, and tax treatment may differ for the

107

purchase of gold coins. Most gold coins are sold purely for their gold content, such as the U.S. gold Eagle, but others, mainly those that originally were minted for circulation, can sell for more than their gold content alone, due to their rarity and/or condition. Such "numismatic" coins fluctuate in value far more than do standard mint coins and may not always trade in a deep market (*i.e.*, with a large spread between bid and asked). Gold bullion, whether held in the form of wafers or bars, provides another option for gold investors, but such holdings may necessitate the expense and delay of an assay before they can be sold.

There are many ways to invest in gold indirectly. More sophisticated investors may invest in gold through options and futures markets. But these markets involve the added risk of leverage (thus a decline in the gold price brings margin calls on long positions) and are not always sufficiently liquid (thus lowering the chances of obtaining a fair price). Gold mining shares are another way to invest in gold indirectly. There are many more risks involved in such shares besides fluctuations in the gold price. A gold mining company must be successful in the exploration, extraction, and distribution of gold if its stock is to appreciate. The way gold mining companies are financed also affects the performance of their stocks. Share prices are more volatile the greater is a mining company's use of leverage (debt). In addition, companies that mine gold often mine other materials as well. Thus a mining stock does not necessarily offer a "pure play" on gold. Gold mutual funds are another indirect vehicle for investing in gold. As with other mutual funds, investors own shares in the fund, not in gold itself. Gold mutual funds invest in gold, bullion, gold mining shares, or a mix of each. Most of these funds offer a safe and convenient method for investors to participate in gold price trends.

Gold also may be used as backing for debt instruments, through a "gold clause" option. A gold clause commits a borrower to repay a paper currency debt in its gold equivalent. Thus, for example, one may borrow $10,000 for 10 years at a time when the price of gold is $300 per ounce. If by the 10th year the price of gold has doubled to $600 per ounce, the principal amount owed on the paper dollar loan also is doubled, to $20,000. The lender is thereby repaid in constant purchasing power. Borrowers are willing to borrow with gold clauses because the interest rate paid on such loans is substantially lower. Why? Interest rates reflect not only credit risk, but an inflation premium. Lenders can demand (and borrowers are willing to pay) higher interest rates if money is cheaper when it is repaid than when it was borrowed. But the purchasing power of gold tends not to change much over long periods of time. Thus interest rates for a gold-denominated loan reflect only a borrower's credit risk. Many U.S. gold mining companies have borrowed in this manner, at interest rates of 3 percent and even less. Other corporations have done the same, issuing gold or silver-denominated, publicly traded bonds.

Gold clauses were common in the United States in the 19th century and before 1933, when they were outlawed by the U.S. Government as part of its default on the gold exchange standard (which was upheld in the Supreme Court). Gold clauses were legalized again in 1977, but their legal status remains unclear. For example, a gold clause may go beyond merely stipulating that repayment be with the gold equivalent in currency, and contain the promise to pay gold itself. This type of clause is rare and not court-tested under today's legal tender laws, which say that an offer of paper dollars is sufficient to satisfy a debt. If a borrower under a gold clause requiring the delivery of physical gold fails to deliver gold and instead offers to repay the debt with paper dollars, the courts probably would rule that the debt was paid, rather than insist on gold and call into question the legal tender status of the U.S. paper dollar. Still, the availability of the gold clause gives borrowers and lenders the opportunity once again to anchor their transactions to gold.

Are You as Smart as a French Peasant?

From the gold investor's point of view, there is a crucial distinction between taking physical possession of gold and holding claims on gold (deposit accounts, mining shares, gold loans, etc.). Unlike Europeans and Asians, Americans have experienced more than 2 centuries of relative stability under a Constitution with a Bill of Rights. Americans, therefore, may be forgiven for often overlooking this distinction. For countless others it has literally meant the difference between life and death.

The difference is this: claims on gold can be taken from you with the "stroke of a pen," because they perforce involve written promises of one sort or another. (Some promises become worthless in the context of a legal and social breakdown.) In contrast, for government officials, or anyone else, to take, say, gold coins from you they will have to, in the final analysis, "prise them out of your cold, dead hand" provided, of course, they know you have them in the first place.

The peasant cited in the subtitle to this section has a cynicism based on experience — the French paper currency has become worthless or nearly worthless on several occasions in modern history. As a result, it is common for French families of all levels of income and wealth to have a stash of gold in their possession. They do so not to get rich — gold pays no income — but to have a irreducible base of wealth and liquidity that may be called upon if needed. Gold is the ultimate insurance policy for those facing a dying economic system. However, gold alone has no value if it cannot ultimately be transferred to a more prosperous setting.

109

The relatively spectacular gains accruing to those holding gold and gold-related investments during the 1970s mainly reflected the severe undervaluation of gold that developed as the gold price was held at $35 per ounce while inflating proceeded during the 1950s and 1960s. As indicated in Chart 10 on p. 129 (Appendix A), the initial surge in the gold price after the collapse of the Bretton Woods system in 1971brought the purchasing power of gold from the bottom to the top of the range that has prevailed when currencies usually were convertible into gold, or, if convertibility were impaired, governments were committed to its restoration.

During the latter half of the 1970s, it became apparent that no government in the world had any intention of restoring convertiblity and that all were, in fact, flaunting their rejection of gold, and price inflation soared to "double digit" rates in nearly every country of the world. In these circumstances, the price of gold was bid up to levels that brought its purchasing power to roughly double its highs of the preceding 2 centuries or so (again, see Chart 10 on p. 129). Since the 1980 peak, the price of gold has decreased irregularly and its purchasing power has returned toward the upper portion of its historic range.

Those who now wish to purchase gold, or who now hold gold, cannot expect to experience a repetition of the spectacular gains of the early 1970s. A repeat of the experience of the late 1970s is conceivable, but the major benefits of holding gold at this time are its traditional ones — impossibility of default and assured liquidity — that have been its major attractions through the ages.

Relative Returns from Gold and Financial Assets

How has gold performed as an investment since currencies became unhinged in late 1971? In the 2 decades or so since then, the dollar price of gold has risen more than tenfold from $35 per ounce to about $375 per ounce today. That appreciation in gold is simply the "other side of the coin," reflecting dollar depreciation. Since physical gold earns no interest, the total return for investments in physical gold arises exclusively from changes in the gold price upward (capital gains) or downward (capital losses).

The annual compounded return on gold from 1971 to 1994 has been about 10.4 percent. Since the U.S. Consumer Price Index has risen roughly 6 percent per year, on average, over that same period, gold returns on an inflation-adjusted basis have been about 4 percent.

However, gold's performance has been volatile, reflecting the volatility of the paper dollar. During the years 1971 through 1994, gold had negative returns half the time (12 years), decreasing in dollar terms by an average of about 12 percent per year during those years. During the 12 years that the dollar price of gold increased (again, from year-end to year-end), it increased at about 38 percent per year. Returns on gold reversed themselves (going from positive to negative, or vice versa) one-third of the time. As discussed above, most of the gains were recorded during the 1970s and most of the losses were recorded in the late 1980s and 1990s.

The lesson to be learned is that gold performs best as a long-term investment. Investors with shorter-term horizons can succeed only by anticipating the shifting sands of government monetary credibility, investing in gold before inflating is high or rising (as in the 1970s) and selling it before disinflation takes hold (as in the mid-1980s and early 1990s).

Gold mining shares also have performed well since 1971. In the decade before 1971, gold mining companies did poorly because they received a fixed price for each ounce of gold sold ($35), while trying to combat the higher material, labor, and interest costs associated with higher price inflation. Between 1971 and 1993, however, the Standard and Poor's index of publicly traded gold mining shares increased by a compounded annual rate of 13.3 percent. Meanwhile, the annual compounded total returns on large-cap stocks and long-term government bonds between 1971 to 1993 have been 11.7 percent and 9.5 percent, respectively (Ibbotson, 1994, pp. 252, 264). Thus gold and gold mining shares have outperformed government bonds since 1971, while gold mining shares, but not physical gold, have outperformed stocks. In sum, with a large assist from gold's severe undervaluation at the start of the period, gold performed well during the past 25 years or so, but with wide swings due to its close connection to gyrations in the value of the paper dollar.

Misconceptions About Gold's Investment Performance

Common misconceptions about gold's performance as an investment stem from misunderstandings about the factors that drive the gold price. Those who mistakenly believe that the gold price is determined by the annual production of gold, or by jewelry demand, or by the emotionalism of "gold bugs," do not understand gold and would not be comfortable investing in it. Others have derided gold because it appears so volatile, does not generate current income, and does not always outperform financial assets over shorter time intervals. There are good reasons for this result that reflect gold's main role. Gold is, first and foremost, money. Only secondarily is gold an investment.

As we have seen, gold has been money through the ages and the notion that it could be a source of income or gains is quite recent. Gold's value has been based on its service as a medium of exchange, a standard of value, and a store of wealth. Gold money alone cannot create wealth. Only free, intelligent, productive human beings can do that. Gold money permits the industrious to produce more abundantly than they would otherwise, using other kinds of money. Whenever gold is prohibited by law to be money, its investment performance will be determined exclusively by fluctuations in the value of forced paper money. Gold will tend to retain its purchasing power under all conditions. Investors cannot expect gold to outperform all other asset classes as an investment under all circumstances. If they do, they misunderstand the primary function of gold. As the great banker, J. P. Morgan, told the Pujo Commission in 1913: Gold is money, and nothing else.

Gold in Personal and Institutional Portfolios

The fact that gold is the "Rock of Gibraltar" of all asset classes, in terms of the stability of its real value over long periods of time, means that it serves best as an anchor, insurer, and diversifier of investment portfolios. In periods of paper money inflation, such as the 1970s, financial assets such as stocks and bonds will do badly or less well, and gold will do very well. In periods of disinflation, such as the 1980s, financial assets will outperform gold. In technical jargon, the price of gold is either negatively correlated or at least not highly correlated with returns from financial assets.

Thus, the addition of gold or gold-equivalent investments to individual and institutional portfolios reduces the volatility of total returns. Putting the point differently, risk-adjusted total returns from portfolios that contain gold will be higher than those without gold. That is a clear investment benefit. In today's climate of fluctuating paper money therefore, every fiduciary dedicated to serving the best interests of beneficiaries would do well to include gold in the construction of portfolios.

IX.

THE FUTURE OF GOLD

THE quarter-century experiment with fiat paper that governments have been engaged in since the breakdown of Bretton Woods in 1968-71 has been an utter failure. As the powers of central banking have been enlarged, the quality of government money has deteriorated badly and government transfer payments, debts, and tax burdens have increased. What solutions suggest themselves? Can fiat money be managed effectively? If not, can the world return to a gold standard? Can banks ever be freed? What prospects exist for gold? Can it have a future as money, beyond its present role as a hedge against the ravages of government monetary malpractice?

Can Fiat Money Be Managed Effectively?

The major lesson to be drawn from the failures of central planning is that it cannot be "reformed." Its problems will not be solved by finding better, more astute, more conscientious planners. The only credible reform is to stop planning and allow producers and consumers to interact freely. The same applies to the central planning of money and banking.

Keynesian economists are in no position to oppose central banking and fiat paper money, let alone reform it. They want central banks to have full discretion to do whatever they wish and they believe that inflating can create jobs. The monetarists, for all their alleged respect for free markets, are no more likely to do so either. They are opponents of fixed exchange rates and the gold standard, and defenders of central banking. Attempts to "overhaul" the Federal Reserve and subject it to rules — an approach endorsed by monetarists for decades — are futile. Worse, this approach conveys the false impression that central banking is legitimate and can somehow be made to "work" with the right policies or the right people. Central banking's only "success" over the years has been financing unlimited government. Central banking and fiat money cannot be managed effectively and are no part of a genuine free market economy (Salsman, 1993).

If the monetary system is to gravitate toward free markets, Keynesians and monetarists will not help. The most promising economists today are those in the new classical school, who argue that central banking is harmful if not ineffectual (Robert Barro), those in the supply-side school, who advocate the classical gold coin standard (Robert Mundell), and those in the Austrian school, who stress the need for both free banking and a gold coin standard (Lawrence White). These economists and their followers represent the vanguard of monetary thinking. They understand that free markets work in money and banking.

The U.S. Gold Commission

Since the abandonment of gold-backed money in 1971, the U.S. Government officially considered a return to gold only when a Congressional "Gold Commission" was formed in 1981-82. A number of factors contributed to forming the Commission. President Reagan and some of his allies in Congress had long been defenders of the gold standard. The rate of price inflation, interest rates, and unemployment rates in the United States had just reached record levels. International agencies such as the World Bank and the IMF were seeking additional monies from the U.S. Congress to transfer to profligate "third world" governments. Certain U.S. Congressman voted for the IMF quota on the condition that a Gold Commission be formed to explore the future role of gold in the international monetary system. They were trying to get to the root of monetary problems.

The Commission amassed considerable data about the history of the gold standard and the paper money standard since 1971 (U.S. Gold Commission, 1982). Witnesses were called to oppose or endorse particular proposals for returning to gold. In a number of ways the final recommendation of the Gold Commission — to do nothing other than instruct the U.S. Treasury to mint gold coins once again — was set in advance. As one consulting firm observed at the time, the majority of the Commission's members convened not to study gold but to bury it (H. C. Wainwright Economics, 1981).

Included on the 17-member panel were the U.S. Secretary of the Treasury (Regan), three Federal Reserve governors (Partee, Rise, Wallich), two monetarist economists (Jordan, Weidenbaum), the chief economic advisor to President Nixon when he abandoned gold in 1971 (McKracken), the head of a commodity firm (Coyne), and assorted Congressmen opposed to gold (Dodd, Wylie, Neal, Reuss, etc.). Each of these members had good reason to oppose gold and avoid blame for the evident monetary debacle. They worked in the very government institutions that helped bring it about.

The research staff of the Commission was headed by a monetarist, Anna Schwartz, long recognized as a fervid opponent of the gold standard and defender of central banking. The research staff highlighted the alleged shortcomings of the gold standard without ever identifying the interventionist origins of those shortcomings. Only Representative Ron Paul and businessman Lewis Lehrman endorsed a gold standard — and had to do so in a separately written minority report (1982).

Can the World Return to a Gold Standard?

Monetary history is fairly clear about what has worked and what has not worked in the past. Both theoretical and historical evidence support the conclusion that free banking and the gold standard deliver the high-quality money and credit appropriate to a free enterprise system. Private incentives lead to constructive outcomes. Markets work, even in money and banking. Central banking and fiat paper money, on the other hand, tend to undermine monetary systems and the efficiency of markets. They do so because fundamentally they are statist arrangements devoid of economic justification, fitted to funding the welfare state and redistributing wealth, not creating it. Given this evidence, economists, legal scholars and statesmen should defend free market money on its own merits, with confidence.

Greenspan (1981) has doubted whether the United States can return to a gold standard. Nevertheless, he cites the high price of gold and cautions against a return to gold that might further drain the Government's gold reserve. He has argued that it would be better to return to a gold standard when price inflation is under control, but adds that a return to gold under such circumstances would be unnecessary, because it would mean that central banking had replicated the results of a gold standard. This argument amounts to saying there are no conditions under which the United States should return to a gold standard, *i.e.*, whether a central bank is being responsible or not, it should never be disciplined by gold. The problems with this are obvious. A gold drain is a sign that the banking system (or an individual bank) is inflating and should stop. The gold standard did not deliver low inflation for some brief period — over sustained periods it delivered *no* inflation or deflation. Greenspan has turned on its head his earlier argument that free banking and the gold standard are the only genuine components of a free market monetary system. He was right the first time.

In contrast to Greenspan, Mundell (1981) finds that gold would serve well as money into the next century. He advocates a gold coin standard and argues, correctly, that:

> If there is a stable international money, there is no conflict between fixed exchange rates and the goal of internal price stability for a single nation state. Under fixed exchange rates, the price level of the individual nation state has to converge to the price level of the world as a whole ... I see no political barriers to [the adoption of a gold standard] if economists can overcome their present love affair with flexible exchange rates, indefinable monetary aggregates [monetarists] and the unemployment approach to stopping inflation [Keynesians]. (Mundell, 1981.)

For all its advantages, Mundell's plan for a return to a gold standard still includes a role for central banks. He insists a gold standard can be managed by central banks so long as they do not monetize government deficits. Neither logic nor history supports this view.

Economists would do well to become more aware of the argument for

115

free banking and become willing to challenge the political status of central banking. All evidence suggests that central banking is a purely discretionary institution whose primary purpose is statist. Central banking's association with the gold standard was purely transitory in this century. The two institutions were like ships passing in the night, with central banking on the rise and gold on the decline, reflecting the rise of central planning and the decline of freedom for markets. Central banking needs to be challenged precisely because it is a political institution that is no part of a free market economy. Lawrence White makes clear why a gold standard must be operated by a free banking system:

> The gold standard, which Keynes once derided as a "barbarous relic," has attracted new attention as a device for limiting the discretion of central banks. There is no question that a commitment to a fixed gold definition of the dollar would anchor the nominal quantity of money, make its purchasing power more predictable, and thereby promote coordination of long-term plans. But as far as damming the source of cyclical monetary disturbances, the gold standard is inadequate without free banking. A central bank tied to gold at a fixed parity can no longer inflate without limit in the long run, but it *can* manipulate in the short run the quantity of high-powered money, and thereby can subject the economy to monetary disruption ... A central bank that has the power to cause monetary disturbances inevitably will cause them. Central bankers, like central economic planners in general, typically lack the incentives and inevitably lack the information necessary for them to perform as skillfully as a market system ... (White, 1989, pp. 160-161.)

If there is ever a return to a gold standard, it will not be accomplished by convening government commissions, which do no real scholarship and are purely bureaucratic undertakings, which perpetuate existing policy. Nor will a gold standard ever be properly managed by central banking, which is inimical to gold. The return to gold will require a sustained intellectual effort from academic economists and monetary reformers who uphold free markets, the gold standard, and free banking. It will require a major shift away from the welfare state that central banks are enlisted to support. Above all, it will require a return to classical liberalism based on a sound philosophic footing of respect for individuals and their right to be as free as possible from coercive government.

Meanwhile, it is encouraging that gold increasingly is in the hands of market participants instead of central banks. Since 1971, investors all over the world have been buying gold in the form of coins, bullion, and gold mining shares, primarily to protect their savings against the ravages of unstable government money. Meanwhile, although central banks and national treasuries continue to sit atop most of the gold they last held as reserves under the Bretton Woods system, they have somewhat reduced their gold holdings via sales and, more significantly, greatly increased their holdings of government debt. Gold now is a far smaller proportion of official reserves than it was in 1971. If these trends persist, the world's central banks will be known solely as repositories of government debt, not of gold.

In 1913, central banks and government agencies held about 30 percent of the world stock of gold. This proportion reached a peak of 62 percent in 1945 before falling back to 30 percent today (see Chart 8). Where is this percentage headed? Central banks and governments as a group tend not to accumulate gold anymore and occasionally they sell it. Meanwhile, the world's gold stock grows 2 percent every year. So the portion of gold held by governments should continue falling, absent a policy shift. With less and less of the total world stock of gold held by central banks and national treasuries, a greater portion is held privately. This was the situation before the rise of central banking. With the legalization of gold ownership and gold clauses, one might envision a return to gold *de facto*.

There are opportunities today for people to use gold. Thus far, this seems to have been limited to gold loans, in which investors who hold gold lend it. The borrowers have been mainly, if not exclusively, gold mining companies, who then sell the borrowed gold, using the proceeds for capital outlays to expand their output. The mining companies are well positioned

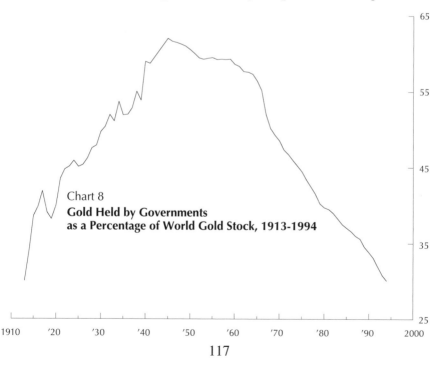

Chart 8
**Gold Held by Governments
as a Percentage of World Gold Stock, 1913-1994**

1910   '20   '30   '40   '50   '60   '70   '80   '90   2000 to devote a portion of their output to repaying the gold they borrowed, and such gold loans generally carry interest rates of 3 percent or less. Gold loans (which have been available to U.S. citizens since it again became legal for them to own gold in 1976), whether private or public, differ little from futures contracts. It is difficult to see how they could become the basis for a return to a classical gold coin standard. However, they do point the way to the low and sustainable interest rates that could be achieved again under gold money.

It has been suggested, notably by former Fed Governor Wayne Angell, that the Treasury issue gold bonds, promising payment in specific amounts of gold, and presumably at a substantially lower interest rate than the Treasury now pays on its promises to pay fiat dollars. Given that the U.S. Government defaulted on its gold clause bonds that were issued early in this century (and that default was upheld by the Supreme Court), it is not at all clear what reception such an issue would receive in the marketplace.

Although there no longer are any legal limitations on using gold in everyday transactions, there are practical difficulties. The foremost of these is the legal tender laws, which make fiat currency the only medium of exchange that the courts will support in satisfaction of debts. These laws mean, among other things, that anyone using gold to purchase or sell things must, at a minimum, do a lot of fancy bookkeeping — every transaction must be converted to fiat dollars using the price of gold at the time. Using the stated value of coins, such as $20 for pre-1933 Double Eagles, or the $50 inscribed on some 1-ounce Eagle coins of recent mintage, or the official price of $42.22 per ounce, would invite a supposition of tax fraud. Thus simply finding other parties willing to use gold in a transaction can be overwhelmingly difficult.

Can Flight from the Paper Dollar Bring Us Back to Gold?

Might some form of hard money standard be adopted in order to salvage a sinking paper dollar? That has happened three times before in U.S. history: first, after the collapse of the Continental currency during the Revolutionary War; second, after the inflationary Greenbacks were issued during the Civil War; and finally, after World War II, when the Bretton Woods gold exchange standard was established. Britain also returned successfully to a gold pound after suspending convertibility for a quarter century during the Napoleonic Wars. Thus there are historical episodes of successful resumptions of sound money. However, intellectual support, not currency crises alone, made such positive reforms possible.

Every fiat paper currency in history has lost its value; those not ultimately rescued by a return to some form of gold convertibility eventually became worthless, such as the French assignat during the French Revolution and the German mark prior to Hitler. History shows that paper currency crises are just as easily followed by dictatorship as they are by enlightened and pro-market reforms. The determining factor is the intellectual climate prevailing before the reforms are undertaken — and whether or not it favors liberty.

There is no doubt that today's U.S. paper dollar is in trouble. Since the United States abandoned the gold-backed dollar in 1971, market confidence in the paper dollar has diminished considerably. We know the paper dollar now is worth only a tenth of its value in terms of gold compared with 1971 (the dollar price of gold has risen by a factor of ten). But the value of the paper dollar has deteriorated even when measured against the purely paper currencies issued by other major governments, such as Japan and Germany. The dollar has fallen from 360 yen in 1971 to under 95 yen more recently, a 74 percent fall. The dollar fell from nearly 4 Deutsche marks in 1971 to under 1.4 recently, a 65 percent drop. For brief periods in between, the dollar has strengthened against gold and these other currencies, but the overall trend clearly is down.

Might this dollar deterioration eventually inspire a return to a gold dollar? Again, only if the intellectual climate is ripe for it. A strong case for limited government and free markets can push reforms in the direction of gold. Crises alone, however, will not do it. Some people still believe crises are "solved" by strong dictators. Nevertheless, compared with the intellectual climate surrounding the severe dollar crisis of the late 1970s, it is clear that today's world is much more respectful of free markets and much more favorable to limiting government. As distrust in the paper dollar persists, respect for gold's underlying stability builds. A return to Constitutional limitations on government generally may lead people to demand a return to the specific monetary provisions the Constitution contains. That role involves government simply defining the dollar in terms of gold, as part of its power to uphold an objective system of weights and measures, and otherwise leaving the market free to choose how many dollars to produce, exchange, and lend. It also involves a return to free banking.

There are practical issues associated with reestablishing the dollar in terms of gold. The last time the dollar was so defined (1971), it was equivalent to 1/35 an ounce of gold; that is, the price of gold was $35 per ounce. Today an ounce of gold is worth about $375, so the dollar is worth considerably less than in 1971, about 1/375 an ounce of gold. This price has fluctuated considerably since 1971, reflecting the arbitrariness of U.S. monetary policy. How should the gold dollar be defined under a new gold standard? If the United States returns the dollar to a gold standard at too low a price, as Britain did in 1925, that risks deflating. If the return to gold is done at too high a price, there is a risk of further inflating (but at least it

119

would be one last burst of inflating unlikely to be repeated once the gold standard was established). Instead of politicians setting the reentry price, it should be set by markets.

What Government must do to assist a resumption of a gold dollar is 1) designate a "resumption date," for example, 6 months into the future; 2) define the dollar in terms of the market price of gold on the resumption date; 3) repeal the legal tender laws mandating that markets accept the paper dollar; and 4) gradually sell off the assets (including gold) of the Federal Reserve and the National Mint. In the period prior to the resumption date, markets would buy and sell gold in anticipation of a future fixed definition of the dollar. This method of reentry would avoid the potential deflation or inflation associated with returning to a gold dollar at too low or too high a price. After resumption, Government still would require that taxes be paid in dollars — but now those dollars would be issued by private banks and convertible into gold at a fixed weight. The Government's public borrowing could continue in private markets, but with no resort to a favored central bank.

Central banking can be phased out without too many practical difficulties. One particular plan envisions a simple sell-off of the assets and liabilities of the Federal Reserve System (Salsman, 1990, Chapter IX). Its major assets would be Government securities and gold coins. These should be transferred to private banks along with the obligation to issue gold-convertible currency in place of inconvertible Federal Reserve notes. As an initial step, the Federal Reserve should cease open-market operations in Government debt, to prepare the ground for a circulation of that debt exclusively in private credit markets. Meanwhile, legal restrictions on private banks should be repealed. These include regulations on ownership, prohibitions on currency issuance, branching and lending decisions, and reserve requirements. Federal deposit insurance should also be abolished in steps (Salsman, 1993b). The only genuine gold standard is a gold coin standard in which depositors can easily demand convertibility of bank currency and deposits. Competitive pressures and a desire for the highest reputation most likely would lead free banks to use gold coin instead of bullion. Bullion banks might well be seen as impeding the convertibility of currency and deposits. Ultimately, even gold coinage could be privatized and the U.S. Mint sold.

The practical benefits of a return to a gold coin standard are significant and numerous. The purchasing power of money would be stabilized. The general level of prices also would stabilize. Interest rates would fall to levels not seen for decades — 1-2 percent for shorter maturities, 3-5 percent for bonds and mortgages — and then stay in that range thereafter. Long-range business planning would be encouraged. The waste associated with private hedging against inflating, fluctuating interest rates, and gyrating exchange rates could be avoided. The banking system would strengthen. Capital markets would deepen (more private borrowing and investing) and lengthen (longer maturities, further encouraging long-range planning). Government would have to balance its budget instead of monetizing its debt. Budget balance would most likely be achieved by lower spending, not higher taxes, since the latter route is neither economically sound nor politically popular. Central banking could no longer be used to disguise or deflect the burdens of the gargantuan state.

Far from being a constraint on economic growth, as the inflationists argue, a gold standard helps make economic prosperity possible. There is overwhelming evidence for this principle in economic history. In addition, there are a number of instances in which fiat paper money has been replaced explicitly by gold money. Reynolds (1984) has examined five such episodes. In each, the return to gold brought sustained economic boom. The first was the establishment of the American dollar in 1792. The ensuing decades were prosperous ones for the United States. The second was Britain's return to gold in 1821, after a 24-year suspension during the Napoleonic Wars. During the suspension, Britain suffered bouts of price inflation and deflation, and depression. After the resumption of gold convertibility, Britain resumed the economic boom it had enjoyed in the 18th century.

The third instance of gold resumption was in the United States after the Civil War. The Greenback Era of inconvertible paper money, from 1862-1879, was a period of chronic instability and recession. The law passed in 1875 announcing a return to the gold standard by January 1, 1879 restored the gold standard without difficulty, and it was followed again by a noninflationary economic boom — America's industrial revolution. The fourth was Britain's return to gold in 1925, after suspending convertibility during World War I. Real per capita income had fallen by 1.3 percent from 1914 to 1924, then rose 14.5 percent from 1925 to 1934. Unemployment fell from 17 percent in 1921 to 9.7 percent in 1929 but did not drop much further, mainly as a reflection of lavish unemployment benefits. The fifth episode, with similarly favorable results, involved France's return to gold in 1926. Unfortunately, the mismanagement of central banks during the Great Depression brought both the British and French resumptions to an end.

Thus, there are a number of important historical instances of countries returning to a gold standard after a lengthy episode of fiat paper money. Economic expansion after World War II also may have been partly attributable to a return to gold under the Bretton Woods system, despite that system's weakness. Crucial lessons can be learned and can guide future monetary reforms. The most successful instance of resumption that we have seen — Britain in 1821 and the United States in 1879 — occurred when central banks were relatively powerless (Britain) or nonexistent (the United States). The least successful resumptions were undertaken in this century, by central banks with vastly increased powers, and did not last very long. The best option for the United States today, following a quarter century of fiat paper money, is a return to a gold coin standard operated by a free banking system. There is no sense in turning back to a confused mix of markets and planning, of gold and central banking, as under Bretton Woods. Nor do we need the gold exchange standard, as operated by the Federal Reserve and other central banks before and during the Great Depression. Any reform short of free banking and the gold coin standard ultimately will prove to be a failure and a disappointment.

The Prospects for Gold and Liberty

The fall of the Berlin Wall in 1989 and the collapse of the Soviet Union in 1991 are universally interpreted as symbols of the failure of government planning and socialism. Since 1980, U.S. voters have favored lower taxes, freer markets, and more limited government, with little care as to which political parties or candidates deliver these results. When politicians fail to carry out their promises to scale back government, they are summarily dismissed. The intellectual-legal-political context required for free banking and the gold standard is still far from being attained. For all the grumblings against the welfare state, it continues to grow and shows no signs of abating, let alone reversing. Few politicians are prepared yet to abolish cabinet agencies or privatize Social Security. Such changes, however, may occur if the trend toward freedom continues. Think tanks have prepared many plans to dismantle government, should the necessary intellectual climate develop. Similar plans exist to return to a genuine gold standard.

Free banking and the gold standard require a context of greater political freedom. All over the world, people have been protesting against big government and voting for freer political systems. If the growing resentment of the failures of central planning and the growing respect for free markets grow further, free market money may be possible one day. The factual evidence of its past performance is a matter of public record — it must be taken seriously by monetary reformers. What is needed above anything else is a clear and unequivocal endorsement of the classical liberal philosophy held by America's Founding Fathers. The prospects for free banking and gold money depend ultimately on the prospects for liberty.

Appendix A

THE RISE AND FALL OF THE U.S. DOLLAR

THE history of the U.S. dollar is a storied one. At the outset it was defined in terms of fixed weights of silver and gold. Today, the dollar is not fixed in terms of any commodity. The trustworthiness of the gold dollar far exceeded that of the paper dollar.

In Colonial times many items circulated as purchasing media, from tobacco to gold. Even the precious metals that served as media of exchange included a wide variety of coins in various conditions of wear and tear. Among these was the Spanish milled dollar. This silver coin was also known as the "pillar dollar" (because of its design), or a "piece of eight" (because its denomination was 8 *reales*). When the Continental Congress considered problems of raising and disbursing funds, its resolutions usually specified these dollars. The rejection of English monetary units presumably reflected the fact that the Spanish coin then was the most widely circulated and trusted coin in America.

Plans for minting Continental currency never progressed past the making of patterns, and the "Continental" was entirely a paper currency promising payment in Spanish milled dollars. Large issues by Congress, and counterfeiting of them by the British, quickly drove the Continental to a discount. At one point, as many as 500 or even 1,000 Continentals may have exchanged for one Spanish milled dollar. The U.S. Government eventually offered to redeem the Continental currency at the rate of one dollar for 100 of the old issue, but only a small fraction was so redeemed. Presumably, most of the remainder had been discarded by its owners as virtually worthless. This episode henceforth made Americans suspicious of banks in general and of currency not linked to gold or silver.

The effects of the collapse of the Continental currency are easily overrated. Many holders of Continentals suffered losses, but apparently there were few debts denominated in Continentals other than the issues themselves. The colonists were used to near-chaos in currency matters, and for the most part they were able to put the Continental in perspective with paper money issued by the states, wampum, pelts, strange coins, etc. During the time of the Continental dollar, much business continued to be transacted in specie (monetary metal), and legal tender laws proved to be unenforceable. General Washington himself instructed the manager of his estates to accept rents only at "intrinsic worth," and he later noted that the law could never "have been intended to make a man take a shilling or sixpence in the pound for a just debt."

Quite clearly, the Spanish milled dollar, not the Continental, was the ancestor of the present U.S. dollar. The Spanish coin remained in circulation in the United States until well into the 19th century, and it was legal tender until 1857. Today its footprints still are visible in the practice of trading securities in fractions of eighths instead of decimals and in the reference to 25 cents as "two bits."

The U.S. dollar was established in 1792 when the Congress authorized the minting of coins with the specifications shown in the table below. The weight of the "dollar or unit," set at 371.25 grains of fine (.995 pure) silver, was determined from an estimate of the approximate average silver content of the "pillar dollar" then in circulation in the United States. (The silver content of individual coins varied because of wear and differences in mintings at Seville, Mexico City, Potosi, etc., but apparently most circulated at par with one another.) The new fractional silver coins were exactly proportional in silver content to the dollar, or unit, and the gold content of the gold coins also was exactly proportional at a ratio of 15 silver to 1 gold. For example, the gold weight of the $10 eagle was exactly two-thirds (10/15) the silver weight of the one dollar, or unit. This 15:1 ratio was presumed to be the market rate of exchange between silver and gold.

The copper weights of the cent and half cent also were originally designed to reflect commodity value, but this proposed "trimetalism" was never implemented. The copper coins' weights were reduced before any

UNITED STATES COINAGE
AUTHORIZED BY THE MINT ACT OF APRIL 2, 1792

Gold Coins	Face Value	Metal Content*
Eagle	$10.00	247.5000
Half eagle	5.00	123.7500
Quarter eagle	2.50	61.8750
Silver Coins		
Dollar or unit	1.00	371.2500
Half dollar	.50	185.0250
Quarter dollar	.25	92.8125
Disme (dime)	.10	37.1250
Half disme (nickel)	.05	18.5025
Copper Coins		
Cent	.01	164.0000†
Half cent	.005	132.0000†

* In grains.

† Reduced to 208 grains for the copper cent and 104 grains for the half cent by Act of January 14, 1793.

Note: Gold coins were an alloy eleven parts fine to one part silver-copper alloy and silver coins were an alloy 1,485 parts fine to 179 parts copper. The weights shown in the table are fine weight only.

were issued, with the result that the mint could purchase copper to be made into coins having a face value larger than the cost of the metal. The profit accrued to the Treasury as "seignorage." In recognition of their lack of commodity value, copper coins were legal tender only for relatively small debts (for those less than $5), and purchases of copper by the mint were limited to specifically authorized amounts. In contrast, the mint was not authorized to buy any specific amount of gold or silver. Gold and silver coins were minted only when private citizens brought bullion or foreign coins to the mint for that purpose.

Thus, original U.S. coins had a specific weight of gold or silver in them. This mint policy of "bimetalism" soon encountered the problem that the market exchange ratio differed from the silver-gold ratio fixed in coins. The problem arose from Government's attempt to fix the price between silver and gold. Such a fixing is unnecessary — and potentially harmful — to free market money. However accurate may have been the Founding Fathers' estimate of the market ratio in 1792, it soon developed that gold eagles could be exchanged for more, say, pounds sterling in London than for the equivalent face value of U.S. silver coins. Therefore, gold bullion and the few U.S. gold coins that were minted were exported, and hardly any gold coins remained in circulation in the United States. Interestingly, U.S. silver dollars also were exported, apparently because they were somewhat lighter than the "pillar dollars" then circulating in Spanish areas where the U.S. issue was accepted at par. Only fractional silver U.S. coins stayed in the country, and, as noted earlier, the Spanish coin remained the principal dollar coin in use here for many years. The silver dollar predominated in early U.S. circulation.

Mint Ratio Altered

This situation prevailed until the 1830s. In 1834 the gold content of the eagle was decreased by Congress to 232 grains of fine gold. The new mint price was $20.67 per troy ounce, reflecting a 6.18 percent devaluation from the $19.34 set in 1792. This change resulted in a slight overvaluation of gold in relation to silver. The flows discussed above were reversed. Gold imports, combined with increased domestic gold production, brought gold coins into general circulation in the United States during the 1840s and 1850s. Thereafter the gold dollar predominated.

In 1853, after many fractional coins had been exported, their silver content was decreased to the rate of 345.6 grains per dollar, but the silver dollar remained 371.25 grains. The U.S. Mint was authorized to purchase limited amounts of silver bullion for the fractional silver coins and to issue such coins at a profit, as with the copper cents. "Free coinage," coinage initiated by private citizens' bringing metal to the mint, remained in effect

125

for the silver dollar at 371.25 grains. But few silver dollars were issued, and the coin fell into disuse.

By design, the Coinage Act of 1873 made no provision for the minting of the silver dollar. Without the guarantee of free coinage, the price of silver fell below the "mint price" of $1.29 per ounce. Subsequent legislation authorized resumed mintings of silver dollars, but it did not authorize resumption of their free coinage. Consequently, the silver dollar became a subsidiary coin whose commodity value was less than its purchasing power.

Through 1873, the difficulties of "bimetalism" were resolved by reducing the metal content of the undervalued coins — gold or silver. After 1873, gold became the premier monetary commodity, and there were no further devaluations until President Franklin D. Roosevelt's "New Deal."

Shortly after taking office, President Roosevelt suspended convertibility of U.S. currency obligations into gold (all other bank-related payments also were suspended for a brief period), ordered U.S. persons to deliver their gold coin and bullion to the Government, and subsequently raised the "price" of gold to $35 per ounce. This new price was paid only to domestic miners and foreigners who sold gold to the Treasury. Other U.S. citizens and persons could not legally hold gold bullion or nonnumismatic coins in the United States. One of the last acts of President Eisenhower was to proscribe gold ownership overseas.

In 1964 the silver content of newly minted U.S. subsidiary coins was eliminated and replaced by a cupronickel "sandwich" (except for the half-dollar, which contained a reduced amount of silver until 1970). In 1967 the U.S. Government discontinued sales of silver at the mint price, and the price of silver subsequently rose above $1.29 per ounce.

In 1968 the Treasury refused to redeem dollar claims (sell gold) at $35 per ounce to anyone except foreign official institutions. As a result, miners, licensed users, and private foreigners paid and received a higher, market-determined price. Finally, in August 1971, the United States closed the "gold window" even to foreign official institutions. The official "price" of gold was increased to $38 per ounce in 1972 and to $42.22 per ounce in 1973. But as some droll commentators have noted, the official "price" today is the price at which the *United States refuses to redeem paper dollars*.

At the turn of the year 1975, Americans again could legally own and hold gold in any form. On January 6th of that year and from time to time thereafter until November 1, 1979, the U.S. Treasury sold a total of 17,053,900 ounces of gold at 21 "auctions." For all sales, the paper dollar price received by the U.S. Treasury for the gold was markedly above the official "price," a "price" that is meaningless as an expression of exchange value.

A Unique Episode

Clearly, the U.S. dollar originally was a specified amount of gold or silver in minted coins. For most of the Nation's history, a dollar claim could be exchanged for *at least* 371.25 grains of silver. Sometimes a dollar could be exchanged for a much larger weight of silver, but only during the past *28 years* of the 203 years since the United States has had its own monetary unit, has a dollar been exchangeable for markedly less than 371.25 grains of silver. Currently a paper dollar can buy about 75 grains of silver.

Similarly, the dollar also has been a specific weight of gold.* Before 1971, dollar obligations were explicit or implicit promises to deliver specific amounts of gold. But now, as during other periods when specie payments were suspended, irredeemable paper dollar claims exchange at a discount to their officially declared gold value. Today, a paper dollar can be exchanged for only about 11 percent its officially stated gold weight.

The Paper Dollar

Far from being consistent with the historical experience of this country, the current paper currency period is a unique episode in U.S. monetary history, as Chart 9 suggests. These purchasing power figures reflect changes in the Producer Price Index (formerly called the Wholesale Price Index), which is only one possible measure of purchasing power. (Another is the Consumer Price Index.) As the chart shows, what a dollar could buy has fluctuated throughout its history — down during some periods (when prices generally were rising) and up during others (when prices generally were falling). The periods of major purchasing power losses were associated with wars. In this respect the dollar's loss of buying power during the 1940s was not unusual.

By the late 1970s there was an incipient "flight from the dollar" into selected other currencies (perceived to provide more buying-power protection than the dollar) and into gold. As Chart 10 reveals, the purchasing power of gold rose to far above even the upper bound of its historical range, as wealth holders sought protection from highly risky paper money and other Government actions hostile to private wealth creation and preservation.

The large drop in the purchasing power of gold since 1980 (evident in Chart 10) indicates that substantial public confidence in the paper dollar

---

* A dollar was 24.75 grains of fine (.995 pure) gold from 1792 to 1834, 23.22 grains from 1834 to 1933, 13.71 grains from 1934 to 1971, 12.63 grains from 1972 to 1973, and 11.37 grains since then. The equivalent gold "prices" per ounce were, respectively, $19.39, $20.67, $35.00, $38.00, and $42.22.

127

and in Government policies toward production of new wealth has been restored. The buying power of gold at the end of 1994 still was close to the

Chart 9
PURCHASING POWER OF THE DOLLAR
(1792 = 1.00)

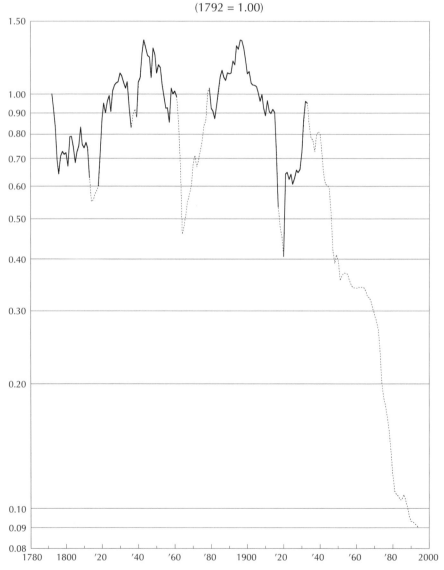

Note: Purchasing power was calculated from the Wholesale Price Index (source: U.S. Department of Labor). The dotted portions of the curve are periods when redeemability of the dollar into the monetary commodities at fixed rates was suspended.

upper bound of its long-term range. This suggested that public confidence and trust remained tenuous. A paper-money system warrants that doubt.

Chart 10
PURCHASING POWER OF GOLD
(1792 = 1.00)

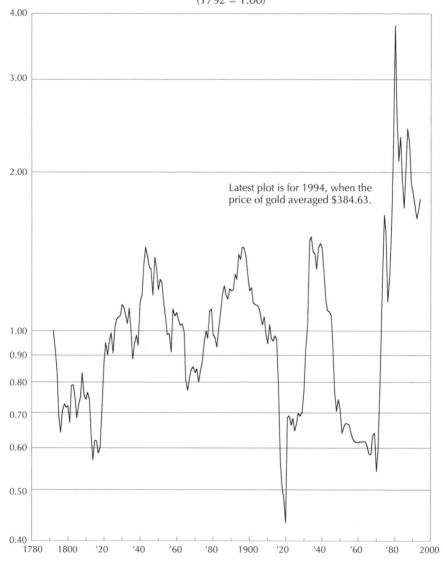

Latest plot is for 1994, when the price of gold averaged $384.63.

Note: The changes in purchasing power shown in the chart were calculated from annual averages of the Wholesale Price Index (source: U.S. Department of Labor) and the annual averages of the exchange ratio of dollars for gold.

129

Sources

I. The Origins of Gold as Money

Angell, Norman. *The Story of Money* (Garden City, NY: Garden City Publishing, 1929).

Anthony, Michael. *The Golden Quest: The Four Voyages of Christopher Columbus* (London: The Macmillan Press, 1992).

Burns, Arthur R. *Money and Monetary Policy in Early Times* (reprint of 1927 edition; New York: Augustus M. Kelley, 1965).

Delmar, Alexander. *Gold Money and Paper Money* (New York: Anson Randolph, 1863).

Desmonde, William. *Magic, Myth and Money* (New York: The Free Press, 1962).

Einzig, Paul. *Primitive Money: Its Ethnological, Historical and Economic Aspects* (London: Eyre and Spottiswoode, 1949).

Frankel, S. Herbert. *Two Philosophies of Money: The Conflict of Trust and Authority* (New York: St. Martin's Press, 1977).

Groseclose, Elgin. *Money and Man: A Survey of Monetary Experience* (Norman, OK: University of Oklahoma Press, 1976).

Hirst, Francis W. *Money: Gold, Silver and Paper* (New York: Charles Scribner's Sons, 1934)

Jevons, William Stanley. *Money and the Mechanism of Exchange* (New York: D. Appleton & Company, 1875/1903).

Keynes, John Maynard. *A Treatise on Money* (London: Macmillan, 1930).

Menger, Carl. "On the Origin of Money," *The Economic Journal*, June 1892, pp. 239-255.

Richards, J. F. *Precious Metals in the Later Medieval and Early Modern Worlds* (Durham: Carolina Academic Press, 1983).

Shaw, W. A. *The History of Currency, 1252-1894* (reprint of 1896 edition; New York: Burt Franklin, 1970).

Skidelsky, Robert. *John Maynard Keynes: The Economist as Savior, 1920-1937* (New York: The Penguin Press, 1994).

Vilar, Pierre. *A History of Gold and Money, 1450-1920* (London: Verso Editions, 1991).

White, Peter T. "The Power of Money," *National Geographic*, January 1993, pp. 80-107.

II. Free Banking and Gold

Barnard, B. W. "The Use of Private Tokens for Money in the United States," *Quarterly Journal of Economics*, 1916-17, pp. 617-626.

Cameron, Rondo (ed.). *Banking in the Early Stages of Industrialization* (Oxford University Press, 1967).

Cameron, Rondo and V. I. Bovykin (ed.). *International Banking, 1870-1914* (Oxford University Press, 1992).

Capie, Forrest and Geoffrey E. Wood (ed.). *Unregulated Banking: Chaos or Order?* (New York: St. Martin's Press, 1991).

Carroll, Charles Holt. *Organization of Debt Into Currency* (reprint of 1858 edition; Van Nostrand Company, 1964).

de Roover, Raymond. *Business, Banking and Economic Thought in Late Medieval and Early Modern Europe* (Chicago: University of Chicago Press, 1974).

Dowd, Kevin. *Laissez-Faire Banking* (London: Routledge, 1993).

Dowd, Kevin. *The Experience of Free Banking* (London: Routledge, 1992).

Glasner, David. *Free Banking and Monetary Reform* (Cambridge University Press, 1989).

Hammond, Bray. "Jackson, Biddle, and the Bank of the U.S.," *The Journal of Economic History*, May 1947.

Humphrey, Thomas M. "The Real Bills Doctrine," *Economic Review*, Federal Reserve Bank of Richmond, September-October 1982.

Kagin, Donald H. *Private Gold Coins and Patterns of the United States* (New York: Arco Publishing Inc., 1981).

Klebaner, Benjamin J. *American Commercial Banking: A History* (New York: Twayne Publishers, 1990).

Mints, Lloyd W. *A History of Banking Theory* (Chicago: University of Chicago Press, 1945).

Rockoff, Hugh. *The Free Banking Era: A Re-Examination* (New York: Arno Press, 1975).

Russell, Steven. "The U.S. Currency System: A Historical Perspective," *Review*, Federal Reserve Bank of St.Louis, September-October 1991.

Salsman, Richard M. "Breaking the Banks: Central Banking Problems and Free Banking Solutions," *Economic Education Bulletin*, Vol. XXX, No. 6, American Institute for Economic Research, June 1990.

Sargent, Thomas J. and Neil Wallace, "The Real Bills Doctrine versus the Quantity Theory: A Reconsideration," *Journal of Political Economy*, 1982.

Sechrest, Larry J. *Free Banking: Theory, History, and a Laissez-Faire Model* (Westport, CT: Quorum Books, 1993).

Selgin, George A. *The Theory of Free Banking: Money Supply Under Competitive Note Issue* (Totowa, NJ: Rowman & Littlefield, 1988).

Selgin, George A. and Lawrence H. White. "How Would the Invisible Hand Handle Money?," *Journal of Economic Literature,* December 1994, pp. 1718-1749.

Smith, Adam. *An Inquiry Into the Nature and Causes of the Wealth of Nations* (1776).

White, Lawrence H. *Free Banking in Britain: Theory, Experience, and Debate, 1800-1845* (Cambridge University Press, 1984).

White, Lawrence H. *Competition and Currency: Essays on Free Banking and Money* (New York: New York University Press, 1989).

White, Lawrence H. (ed.). *Free Banking* (Brookfield, VT: Edward Elgar Publishing, 1993).

III. The Gold Standard in Theory

Barro, Robert J. "Money and the Price Level Under the Gold Standard," *Economic Journal*, March 1979, pp. 13-27.

Bordo, Michael D. and Richard Ellison. "A Model of the Classical Gold Standard With Depletion," *Journal of Monetary Economics*, 1985.

Busschau, William J. *The Theory of Gold Supply* (Oxford University Press, 1936).

Dowd, Kevin. "Financial Instability in a 'Directly Convertible' Gold Standard," *Southern Economic Journal*, January 1991.

Eichengreen, Barry (ed.). *The Gold Standard in Theory and History* (New York: Methuen, 1985).

Friedman, Milton. "Commodity Reserve Currency," in Milton Friedman, *Essays in Positive Economics* (Chicago: University of Chicago Press, 1953).

Friedman, Milton. "Bimetallism Revisited," in Milton Friedman, *Money Mischief: Episodes in Monetary History* (New York: Harcourt Brace, 1992), pp. 126-156.

Garrison, Roger W. "The Costs of a Gold Standard," in Llewellyn H. Rockwell, Jr. (ed.), *The Gold Standard: An Austrian Perspective* (Lexington, MA: D. C. Heath, 1985).

Hardy, Charles O. *Is There Enough Gold?* (Washington, DC: Brookings Institution, 1936).

Hayek, Friedrich A. "A Commodity Reserve Currency," in *Individualism and Economic Order* (Chicago: University of Chicago Press, 1948).

Hotelling, Harold. "The Economics of Exhaustible Resources," *Journal of Political Economy*, 1931.

Hume, David. "Of the Balance of Trade" (1752) in E. Rotwein (ed.), *Writings on Economics* (Salem, NH: Ayer, 1955 reprint).

Jastram, Roy W. *The Golden Constant: The English and American Experience, 1560-1976* (New York: John Wiley & Sons, 1977).

Kemmerer, Donald L. "The Gold Standard and Economic Growth" (Greenwich, CT: Committee for Monetary Research and Education, October 1974).

Lehrman, Lewis E. and Ron Paul. *The Case for Gold: The Minority Report of the U.S. Gold Commission* (Washington, DC: The Cato Institute, 1982).

McCormack, John L. "The Supply and Demand for Gold" (Chicago: Minerals Market Research, 1989).

Pindyck, Robert. "The Optimal Exploration and Production of Nonrenewable Resources," *Journal of Political Economy,* 1978.

Pindyck, Robert and David Levhari. "The Pricing of Durable Exhaustible Resources," *Quarterly Journal of Economics*, 1981.

Rockoff, Hugh. "Some Evidence on the Real Price of Gold, Its Cost of Production, and Commodity Prices," in Michael D. Bordo and Anna J. Schwartz (ed.), *A

Retrospective on the Classical Gold Standard, 1821-1931 (Chicago: University of Chicago Press, 1984).

Rockwell, Llewellyn H., Jr. (ed.). *The Gold Standard: An Austrian Perspective* (Lexington, MA: D. C. Heath & Co., 1985).

Salerno, Joseph. "Gold Standards: True and False," in James A. Dorn and Anna J. Schwartz (ed.), *The Search for Stable Money* (Chicago: University of Chicago Press, 1987).

Schwartz, Anna J. (ed.). *Commodity Monies* (Brookfield, VT: Edward Elgar Publishing, 1992).

Sechrest, Larry J. *Free Banking: Theory, History, and a Laissez-faire Model* (Westport, CT: Quorum Books, 1993).

Sennholz, Hans (ed.). *Gold is Money* (Westport, CT: Greenwood Publishing, 1975).

Skousen, Mark. *Economics of a Pure Gold Standard* (Auburn, AL: Ludwig von Mises Institute, 1988).

von Mises, Ludwig. *The Theory of Money and Credit* (reprint of 1912 edition; Indianapolis: Liberty Classics, 1980).

IV. The Classical Gold Standard

Aghevli, Bijan B. "The Balance of Payments and Money Supply Under the Gold Standard Regime: U.S., 1879-1914," *American Economic Review*, March 1975.

Barrett, Don C. *The Greenbacks and Resumption of Specie Payments, 1862-1879* (Cambridge: Harvard University Press, 1931).

Bloomfield, Arthur I. *Monetary Policy Under the International Gold Standard, 1880-1914* (New York: Federal Reserve Bank of New York, 1959).

Bloomfield, Arthur I. *Short-Term Capital Movements Under the Pre-1914 Gold Standard* (Princeton: Princeton Studies in International Finance #11, 1963).

Bordo, Michael D. and Anna J. Schwartz (ed.). *A Retrospective on the Classical Gold Standard, 1821-1931* (Chicago: University of Chicago Press, 1984).

Bordo, Michael D. "The Classical Gold Standard: Some Lessons for Today," *Review*, Federal Reserve Bank of St. Louis, May 1981, pp. 2-17.

Davidson, James D. "Gold, Not Fiscal Responsibility, Curbed Deficits," *Dollars and Sense*, National Taxpayers Union, June-July 1988.

de Cecco, Marcello. *The International Gold Standard: Money and Empire* (New York: St. Martin's Press, 1984).

Eichengreen, Barry. *Golden Fetters: The Gold Standard and the Great Depression, 1919-1939* (New York: Oxford University Press, 1992).

Fetter, Frank W. *Development of British Monetary Orthodoxy, 1797-1875* (Cambridge: Harvard University Press, 1965).

Gregory, T. E. *The Gold Standard and Its Future* (London: E. P. Dutton, 1935).

Hawtrey, Ralph G. *The Gold Standard in Theory and Practice* (London: Longmans Green & Company, 1939).

Hinderliter, Roger H. and Hugh Rockoff. "Banking Under the Gold Standard: An

Analysis of Liquidity Management in the Leading Financial Centers," *Journal of Economic History*, June 1976, pp. 379-398.

Kaminsky, Graceila L. and Michael Klein. "The Real Exchange Rate and Fiscal Policy During the Gold Standard Period: Evidence from the United States and Great Britain," Working Paper #4809 (Cambridge: National Bureau of Economic Research, Inc., 1994).

Kemmerer, Edwin W. *Gold and the Gold Standard* (New York: McGraw-Hill Company, 1944).

Kindahl, James K. "Economic Factors in Specie Resumption in the United States, 1865-79," *Journal of Political Economy*, February 1961.

McCloskey, Donald N. and J. Richard Zecher. "How the Gold Standard Worked, 1880-1913," in Jacob A. Frankel and Harry G. Johnson (ed.), *The Monetary Approach to the Balance of Payments* (Toronto: University of Toronto Press, 1976).

McCulloch, J. Huston. "Beyond the Historical Gold Standard," in Colin D. Campbell and William R. Dougan (ed.), *Alternative Monetary Regimes* (Baltimore: Johns Hopkins University Press, 1986).

McKinnon, Ronald I. "When Capital Flowed and Exchange Rates Held," *The Wall Street Journal*, March 28, 1988.

"Resumption of Specie Payments," Testimony Before the Committee on Banking and Currency, U.S. House of Representatives (Washington, DC: Government Printing Office, 1878).

Reynolds, Alan. "Gold and Economic Boom: Five Case Studies, 1792-1926," in Barry N. Siegel (ed.), *Money in Crisis* (Cambridge: Ballinger Publishing Company, 1984).

Salsman, Richard M. "Breaking the Banks: Central Banking Problems and Free Banking Solutions," *Economic Education Bulletin*, Vol. XXX, No. 6, American Institute for Economic Research, June 1990.

Schwartz, Anna J. "Alternative Monetary Regimes: The Gold Standard," in Colin D. Campbell and William R. Dougan (ed.), *Alternative Monetary Regimes* (Baltimore: Johns Hopkins University Press, 1986).

Smith, Adam. *An Inquiry Into the Nature and Causes of the Wealth of Nations* (1776).

White, Horace. *The Gold Standard: How It Came to the World and Why It Will Stay* (New York: Evening Post Publishing, 1893).

Zarnowitz, Victor. *Business Cycles: Theory, History, Indicators, and Forecasting* (Chicago: University of Chicago Press, 1992).

V. Political and Legal Issues

Anderson, Benjamin M. *Economics and the Public Welfare* (New York: Van Nostrand, 1949).

Bordo, Michael D. and Finn. E. Kydland. "The Gold Standard as a Rule," Working Paper #9205, Federal Reserve Bank of Cleveland, 1992.

Bordo, Michael D. and Anna J. Schwartz. "The Specie Standard as a Contingent

Rule: Some Evidence for Core and Peripheral Countries, 1880-1990," Working Paper #4860 (Cambridge: National Bureau of Economic Research, Inc., 1994).

Buffett, Howard. "Human Freedom Rests on Gold Redeemable Money," *The Commercial and Financial Chronicle*, May 6, 1948.

Dam, Kenneth W. *The Rules of the Game: Reform and Evolution in the International Monetary System* (Chicago: University of Chicago Press, 1982).

Dodd, Nigel. *The Sociology of Money: Economics, Reason and Contemporary Society* (New York: The Continuum Publishing Company, 1994).

Dunne, Gerald T. *Monetary Decisions of the Supreme Court* (New Brunswick, NJ: Rutgers University Press, 1960).

Flood, Robert P. and Peter M. Garber. "Gold Monetization and Gold Discipline," *Journal of Political Economy*, February 1984.

Frankel, S. Herbert. *Two Philosophies of Money: The Conflict of Trust and Authority* (New York: St. Martin's Press, 1977).

Frankel, S. Herbert. *Money and Liberty* (Washington, DC: American Enterprise Institute, 1980).

Friedman, Milton and Anna J. Schwartz. *A Monetary History of the U.S., 1867-1960* (Princeton: Princeton University Press, 1963).

Getman, Robert S. "Gold and the Founding Fathers,"*The Objectivist Forum,* October 1980.

Greenspan, Alan. "Gold and Economic Freedom," in Ayn Rand (ed.), *Capitalism: The Unknown Ideal* (New York: New American Library, 1967).

Hazlitt, Henry. "Twenty-Three-Cent Dollar, What Four Decades of Inflation Have Wrought," *Barron's*, October 6, 1975.

Holloway, J. D. "Gold Is the Policeman of the Politician," in Charles R. Whittlesey (ed.), *Readings in Money and Banking* (New York: W. W. Norton, 1952), pp. 413-416.

Holzer, Henry Mark. *The Gold Clause* (New York: Books-in-Focus, 1980).

Holzer, Henry Mark. *Government's Money Monopoly* (New York: Books-in-Focus, 1981a).

Holzer, Henry Mark. "How Americans Lost Their Right to Own Gold and Became Criminals in the Process" (Greenwich, CT: Committee for Monetary Research and Education, 1981b).

Homer, Sidney. *A History of Interest Rates: 2000 B.C. to the Present* (reprint of 1963 edition; New Brunswick, NJ: Rutgers University Press, 1993).

Hurst, James W. *A Legal History of Money in the U.S., 1774-1970* (Nebraska University Press, 1973).

Kemmerer, Edwin W., *et al. Money and the Law* (New York University, 1945).

Kemp, Arthur. *The Legal Qualities of Money* (New York: Pageant Press, 1956).

Keynes, John Maynard. *The Economic Consequences of the Peace* (New York: Harcourt Brace, 1920).

Knapp, Georg Friedrich. *The State Theory of Money* (London: Macmillan & Company, 1924).

Madison, James. *The Debates in the Federal Convention of 1787, Volumes I and II* (reprint of 1787 edition; Buffalo: Prometheus Books, 1987).

Madison, James, Alexander Hamilton and John Jay. *The Federalist Papers* (1788).

Mann, F. A. *The Legal Aspect of Money* (New York: Oxford University Press, 1992).

Manne, Henry G. and Roger LeRoy Miller (ed.). *Gold, Money and the Law* (Chicago: Aldine Publishing Company, 1975).

Nussbaum, Arthur. *Money in the Law* (Chicago: The Foundation Press, Inc., 1939).

Rand, Ayn. *Atlas Shrugged* (reprint of 1957 edition; New York: Dutton, 1992).

Redenbaugh, Russell G. "Stable Money is a Moral Commitment," *The Wall Street Journal*, January 14, 1994.

Rothbard, Murray N. *The Mystery of Banking* (New York: Richardson and Snyder, 1983).

Scherman, Harry. *The Promises Men Live By* (New York: Random House, 1938).

Schumpeter, Joseph A. *History of Economic Analysis* (New York: Oxford University Press, 1954).

Siegen, Bernard H. "The Supreme Court Pointed Us Toward Paper Money," *The Wall Street Journal*, June 20, 1984.

Timberlake, Richard H., Jr. *Gold, Greenbacks and the Constitution* (Berryville, VA: The George Edward Durell Foundation, 1991).

Vieira, Edwin, Jr. *Pieces of Eight: The Monetary Powers and Disabilities of the U.S. Constitution* (Greenwich, CT: Devin-Adair, 1983).

Vieira, Edwin, Jr. "Constitutional Authority of the States and the President to Intervene on Behalf of Sound Money" (Greenwich, CT: Committee for Monetary Research and Education, 1983).

Webster, Daniel. "A Redeemable Paper Currency," A Speech Delivered in the U.S. Senate, February 22, 1834, reprinted in Edwin P. Whipple (ed.), *The Great Speeches and Orations of Daniel Webster* (Boston: Little, Brown & Co., 1894).

White, Lawrence H. *Competition and Currency: Essays on Free Banking and Money* (New York: New York University Press, 1989).

VI. Subversion of the Gold Standard

Benjamin M. Anderson, Jr. "The Gold Standard versus 'A Managed Currency,'" *Chase Economic Bulletin*, March 23, 1925.

Bordo, Michael D. "The Gold Standard, Bretton Woods and Other Monetary Regimes: A Historical Appraisal," *Review*, Federal Reserve Bank of St. Louis, March-April 1993.

Brown, William Adams. *The International Gold Standard Reinterpreted, 1914-1934* (Cambridge: National Bureau of Economic Research, 1940).

Cassel, Gustav. *The Downfall of the Gold Standard* (Oxford University Press, 1936).

Cooper, Richard N. "The Gold Standard: Historical Facts and Future Prospects," *Brookings Papers on Economic Activity, Volume 1* (Washington, DC: Brookings Institution, 1982).

Crabbe, Leland. "The International Gold Standard and U.S. Monetary Policy from World War I to the New Deal," *Federal Reserve Bulletin*, June 1989, pp. 423-440.

"Degradation of the Dollar," *Economic Education Bulletin*, Vol. VIII, No. 7, American Institute for Economic Research, September 1968.

Eichengreen, Barry (ed.) *The Gold Standard in Theory and History* (New York: Methuen, 1985).

Eichengreen, Barry. *Golden Fetters: The Gold Standard and the Great Depression, 1919-1939* (Oxford University Press, 1992).

Einzig, Paul. *Will Gold Depreciate?* (Macmillan and Company, 1937).

Faulkner, Harold U. *The Decline of Laissez-Faire, 1897-1917, Volume VII, The Economic History of the U.S.* (Reinhart & Company, Inc., 1951).

Friedman, Milton. "Real and Pseudo Gold Standards," *Journal of Law and Economics*, October 1961.

Friedman, Milton and Anna J. Schwartz. *A Monetary History of the U.S., 1867-1960* (Princeton: Princeton University Press, 1963).

"The Gold Standard Revisited," *The Economist*, March 6, 1993.

Green, Steven L. "The Abrogation of Gold Clauses in 1933 and Its Relation to Current Controversies in Monetary Economics," *Economic Review*, Federal Reserve Bank of Dallas, July 1986.

Hardy, Charles O. *Is There Enough Gold?* (Washington, DC: Brookings Institution, 1936).

Hazlitt, Henry. *From Bretton Woods to World Inflation* (Regnery Gateway, 1984).

Hollis, Christopher. *The Breakdown of Money: An Historical Explanation* (New York: Sheed and Ward, 1934).

Holzer, Henry Mark. *The Gold Clause* (New York: Books-in-Focus, 1981).

Holzer, Henry Mark. "How Americans Lost Their Right to Own Gold and Became Criminals in the Process" (Greenwich, CT: Committee for Monetary Research and Education, June 1984).

Keynes, John Maynard. *A Tract on Monetary Reform* (London: Macmillan & Co., Limited, 1923).

Keynes, John Maynard. *A Treatise on Money* (London: Macmillan & Co., Limited, 1930).

Keynes, John Maynard. "The Economic Consequences of Mr. Churchill" (1925), "The End of Laissez-Faire" (1926), and "The End of the Gold Standard" (1931), in *Essays in Persuasion* (New York: Harcourt, Brace and Co., 1932).

Keynes, John Maynard. *The General Theory of Employment, Interest and Money* (New York: Harcourt, Brace and Co., 1936).

Lehrman, Lewis E. "Gold is Not a 'Side Show,'" *The Wall Street Journal*, February 20, 1980.

Levine, Richard J. and Richard F. Janssen, "As Gold Rises Further, Washington Reaction Becomes More Muted," *The Wall Street Journal*, January 18, 1980.

Mlynarski, Feliks. *Gold and Central Banks* (The Macmillan Company, 1929).

Mlynarski, Feliks. *The Functioning of the Gold Standard* (League of Nations, 1931).

Moggridge, Donald E. *The Return to Gold, 1925* (Cambridge University Press, 1969).

Morgan-Webb, Charles. *The Rise and Fall of the Gold Standard* (New York: The Macmillan Company, 1934).

Mundell, Robert A., *et al.* "The Future of Gold," *American Economic Review, Papers and Proceedings*, May 1969.

Nurske, Ragnar. "The Gold Exchange Standard," in Barry Eichengreen (ed.), *The Gold Standard in Theory and History* (New York: Methuen, 1985).

Palyi, Melchior. *The Twilight of Gold, 1914-1936* (Henry Regnery Company, 1972).

Phillips, C. A., T. F. McManus, and R. W. Nelson, *Banking and the Business Cycle: A Study of the Great Depression in the United States* (The Macmillan Company, 1937).

Pollard, Sidney (ed.). *The Gold Standard and Employment Policies Between the Wars* (London: Methuen and Company Ltd, 1970).

Royal Institute of International Affairs, *The International Gold Problem* (Oxford University Press, 1931).

Salsman, Richard M. "Breaking the Banks: Central Banking Problems and Free Banking Solutions," *Economic Education Bulletin*, Vol. XXX, No. 6, American Institute for Economic Research, June 1990.

Salsman, Richard M. "The Collapse of Deposit Insurance — and the Case for Abolition," *Economic Education Bulletin*, Vol. XXXIII, No. 9, American Institute for Economic Research, September 1993.

Salsman, Richard M. "Did the Gold Standard Cause the Great Depression?," *Research Reports*, American Institute for Economic Research, April 4, 1994a.

Salsman, Richard M. "Making Money When Money Was Gold," H. C. Wainwright & Co. Economics, Inc., October 24, 1994b.

Shelton, Judy. *Money Meltdown: Restoring Order to the Global Currency System* (New York: Free Press, 1994).

Sproul, Allen. "Money Will Not Manage Itself" (New York University, 1963).

Sutton, Antony C. *The War on Gold* (Sandton, Valiant Publishers, 1977).

Walker, Charles H. "The Working of the Pre-War Gold Standard," *The Review of Economic Studies*, Volume 1, 1933-34, pp. 196-209.

Weber, Christopher. ". . . Good as Gold"? How We Lost Our Gold Reserves and Destroyed the Dollar (Berryville, VA: George Edward Durell Foundation, 1988).

Wright, Quincy (ed.). *Gold and Monetary Stabilization* (Chicago: University of Chicago Press, 1932).

VII. Central Banking and Gold

Acres, W. Marston. *The Bank of England From Within, 1694-1931* (London: Oxford University Press, 1931).

Alesina, Alberto and Lawrence H. Summers. "Central Bank Independence and Macroeconomic Performance: Some Comparative Evidence," *Journal of Money, Credit and Banking*, May 1993.

Bagehot, Walter. *Lombard Street* (London: Henry S. King, 1873).

Bloomfield, Arthur I. *Monetary Policy Under the International Gold Standard, 1880-1914* (New York: Federal Reserve Bank of New York, 1959).

Briggs, John, D. B. Christenson, Pamela Martin, and Thomas D. Willet. "The Decline of Gold as a Source of U.S. Monetary Discipline," in Thomas D. Willet (ed.), *Political Business Cycles: The Political Economy of Money, Inflation and Unemployment* (Durham, NC: Duke University Press, 1988).

Brittan, Samuel. "The Zenith of the Central Banks," *Financial Times* (London), June 9, 1994, p. 14.

Burns, Arthur F. "The Anguish of Central Banking," *Federal Reserve Bulletin*, September 1987.

Capie, Forrest H. (ed.). *Major Inflations in History* (Brookfield, VT: Edward Elgar Publishing, 1991).

Collins, Michael (ed.). *Central Banking in History* (Brookfield, VT: Edward Elgar Publishing, 1993).

Eichengreen, Barry. *Golden Fetters: The Gold Standard and the Great Depression, 1919-1939* (New York: Oxford University Press, 1992).

Eichengreen, Barry. "Conducting the International Orchestra: Bank of England Leadership Under the Classical Gold Standard," *Journal of International Money and Finance,* March 1987, p. 5-26.

Fischer, Stanley. "Seignorage and the Case for a National Money," *Journal of Political Economy*, April 1982.

Friedman, Milton. "Government Revenue from Inflation," *Journal of Political Economy*, July-August 1971.

Goff, Brian L. and Mark Toma. "Optimal Seignorage, the Gold Standard, and Central Bank Financing," *Journal of Money, Credit and Banking*, February 1993.

"Gold's Surge Raises Worry of Huge Sales," *The Wall Street Journal*, June 1, 1993, p. C1.

Goodhart, Charles. *The Evolution of Central Banks* (Cambridge: MIT Press, 1988).

Greenspan, Alan. "Gold and Economic Freedom," in Ayn Rand (ed.), *Capitalism: The Unknown Ideal* (New York: New American Library, 1967).

Greenspan, Alan. "The Role of a Central Bank in a Democratic Society," Statement Before the Committee on Banking, Finance and Urban Affairs of the U.S. House of Representatives, October 13, 1993, in *Federal Reserve Bulletin*, December 1993, pp. 1100-1107.

Greider, William. *Secrets of the Temple: How the Federal Reserve Runs the Country* (New York: Simon and Schuster, 1987).

Groseclose, Elgin. *America's Money Machine: The Story of the Federal Reserve* (Westport, CT: Arlington House Publishers, 1980).

Hall, Robert E. (ed.). *Inflation: Causes and Effects* (Chicago: University of Chicago Press, 1982).

Kane, Edward J. "Politics and Fed Policymaking," *Journal of Monetary Economics*, April 1980.

Keynes, John Maynard. *The Economic Consequences of the Peace* (New York: Harcourt, Brace and Howe, 1920).

Lehrman, Lewis E. "The Curse of the Paper Dollar," *The Wall Street Journal*, November 6, 1990.

Lipsey, Richard G. "Government and Inflation," *American Economic Review*, May 1982.

Lipsey, Richard G. "What We Have Learned About Inflation in the Past 300 Years," *Atlantic Economic Journal*, March 1985.

Lohani, Prakash and Earl A. Thompson. "The Optimal Rate of Secular Inflation," *Journal of Political Economy*, September-October 1971.

Nurske, Ragnar. "The Gold Exchange Standard" (1944), reprinted in Barry Eichengreen (ed.), *The Gold Standard in Theory and History* (New York: Methuen, 1985).

Okun, Arthur, *et al. Inflation: The Problems It Creates and the Policies It Requires* (New York: New York University Press, 1970).

Paarlberg, Don. *An Analysis and History of Inflation* (Westport, CT: Praeger Publishers, 1993).

Palyi, Melchior. *An Inflation Primer* (Chicago: Henry Regnery Company, 1962).

Palyi, Melchior. *The Twilight of Gold, 1914-1936* (Chicago: Henry Regnery Company, 1972).

Plender, John. "Disinterested Protectors of the Public Good," *Financial Times* (London), September 30, 1994.

Rockoff, Hugh. "Walter Bagehot and the Theory of Central Banking," in Forrest Capie and Geoffrey E. Wood (ed.), *Financial Crises and the World Banking System* (New York: St. Martin's Press, 1986).

Rueff, Jacques. *The Age of Inflation* (Chicago: Henry Regnery Company, 1964).

Rueff, Jacques. *The Monetary Sin of the West* (The Macmillan Company, 1972).

Salsman, Richard M. "Breaking the Banks: Central Banking Problems and Free Banking Solutions," *Economic Education Bulletin*, Vol. XXX, No. 6, American Institute for Economic Research, June 1990.

Salsman, Richard M. "Can Fiat Money Be Managed Effectively?," *Research Reports*, American Institute for Economic Research, June 7, 1993a.

Salsman, Richard M. "Bankers as Scapegoats for Government-Created Crises in U.S. History," in Lawrence H. White (ed.), *The Crisis in American Banking* (New York: New York University Press, 1993b).

Samuelson, Paul. *Economics: An Introductory Analysis* (New York: McGraw Hill, 1948).

Sayers, R. S. *Central Banking After Bagehot* (Oxford University Press, 1957).

"A Short History of Inflation," *The Economist*, February 22, 1992.

Smith, Vera C. *The Rational of Central Banking and the Free Banking Alternative* (reprint of 1936 edition; Indianapolis: Liberty Press, 1990).

Szenberg, Michael (ed.). *Eminent Economists: Their Life Philosophies* (Cambridge: Cambridge University Press, 1992).

Tallman, Ellis W. "Inflation: How Long Has This Been Going On?," *Economic Review*, Federal Reserve Bank of Atlanta, November-December 1993.

Timberlake, Richard H., Jr. "Monetary Policy's Payoff to the Treasury," *The Wall Street Journal*, December 22, 1986.

Timberlake, Richard H., Jr. *Monetary Policy in the United States: An Intellectual and Institutional History* (Chicago: University of Chicago Press, 1993).

Vaubel, Roland. "The Government's Money Monopoly: Externalities or Natural Monopoly?," *Kyklos*, No. 1, 1984.

Volcker, Paul A. "The Role of Central Banks," in *Central Banking Issues in Emerging Market Economies*, A Symposium Sponsored by the Federal Reserve Bank of Kansas City, 1990.

von Mises, Ludwig. *On the Manipulation of Money and Credit* (Dobbs Ferry, NY: Free Market Books, 1978).

Weigand, G. Carl (ed.). *The Menace of Inflation: Its Causes and Consequences* (Old Greenwich, CT: Devin-Adair, 1977).

White, Lawrence H. "Which Kind of Monetary Policy, If Any?," *The Cato Journal*, Fall 1993.

Williams, Charles E. *The Immorality of Inflation* (New York: Theo. Gauss & Co., 1970).

VIII. Gold as a Barometer and Investment

Baker, Stephen A. and Roger C. van Tassel. "Forecasting the Price of Gold: A Fundamentalist Approach," *Atlantic Economic Journal*, December 1985.

Bernstein, Jacob. *Investing in Metals* (New York: John Wiley & Sons, 1991).

Coin Buyer's Guide (Great Barrington, MA: American Institute for Economic Research, 1990).

Gold 1994 (London: Gold Fields Mineral Services, Ltd., 1994).

Gold in the Institutional Portfolio (New York: World Gold Council, 1991).

The Gold Mine Book (Great Barrington, MA: American Investment Services, Inc., 1990).

"Gold as Money Investment or Speculative Commodity?," *Research Reports*, American Institute for Economic Research, September 19, 1988.

Green, Timothy. *The New World of Gold* (New York: Walker and Company, 1984).

Hoppe, Donald J. *How to Invest in Gold Stocks* (New Rochelle, NY: Arlington House, 1972).

Howe, Reginald H. "The Golden Sextant," *International Currency Prize Essay, 1992* (Zurich: Bank Lips, AG, 1993).

Ibbotson Associates. *Stocks, Bonds, Bills and Inflation, 1926-93* (Chicago, 1994).

Jastram, Roy W. *The Golden Constant: The English and American Experience, 1560-1976* (New York: John Wiley & Sons, 1977).

Kehrer, Daniel M. *Profits in Precious Metals* (New York: Random House, 1985).

Lehrman, Lewis E. "Gold in a Global Multi-Asset Portfolio," Morgan Stanley & Company, March 4, 1988.

Ranson, R. David. "To Know the Future, Watch Gold," *The Wall Street Journal*, November 17, 1990.

Ranson, R. David. "Gold: A Leading Indicator of Financial Market Conditions," *World Gold Review*, World Gold Council, Spring 1992.

Reisman, George. "What Determines the Price of Gold?," *The Intellectual Activist* (1982-83).

Ricardo, David. *The High Price of Bullion: A Proof of the Depreciation of Bank Notes* (London: Murray, 1810. Reprinted in Piero Sraffa, ed., *The Works and Correspondence of David Ricardo*, Volume 3, Pamphlets and Papers, 1809-1811. Cambridge University Press, 1951).

Ritter, Lawrence S. and Thomas J. Ulrich. "The Role of Gold in Consumer Investment Portfolios," New York University Graduate School of Business, 1984.

Salsman, Richard M. "'Armageddon Economics': When is Government Debt Inflationary?," *Economic and Investment Observations,* H. C. Wainwright & Co. Economics, Inc., June 8, 1993.

Salsman, Richard M. "Seeing Gold in a New Vein," *International Gold Mining Newsletter,* May 1994a.

Salsman, Richard M. "What Explains Gold's Forecasting Power?," H. C. Wainwright & Co. Economics, Inc., August 24, 1994b.

Salsman, Richard M. "Making Money When Money Was Gold," H. C. Wainwright & Co. Economics, Inc., October 10, 1994c.

Sherman, Eugene J. *Gold Investment: Theory and Application* (New York: Prentice Hall, 1986).

Sinclair, James E. and Harry D. Schultz. *How You Can Profit from Gold* (Westport, CT: Arlington House, 1980).

Solt, Michael E. and Paul J. Swanson. "On the Efficiency of the Markets for Gold and Silver," *Journal of Business*, July 1981.

Turk, James. "Do Central Banks Control the Gold Market?," *Freemarket Gold & Money Report*, 1994.

Turk, James. "What Factors Determine the Price of Gold?," *Freemarket Gold & Money Report*, 1993.

Welling, Kathryn M. "Why Gold Will Regain Its Lost Luster," *Barron's*, July 15, 1991.

IX. The Future of Gold

Fabra, Paul. "Gold Convertibility is the Key," *The Wall Street Journal*, July 24, 1985.

Friedman, Milton and Anna J. Schwartz. "Has Government Any Role in Money?," *Journal of Monetary Economics*, January 1986.

Friedman, Milton. "The Case for Overhauling the Federal Reserve," in Robert Guttmann (ed.), *Reforming Money and Finance* (Armonk, NY: M. E. Sharpe Inc., 1989).

"The Gold Commission," *The Political Economy in Perspective*, H. C. Wainwright & Co. Economics, Inc., August 15, 1981.

Greenspan, Alan. "Can the U.S. Return to a Gold Standard?," *The Wall Street Journal*, September 1, 1981.

Hanke, Steve H. "The Fed is a Failure, So Let's Get Rid of It," *The New York Times*, August 10, 1992.

Harwood, E. C. "Advantages of Returning to the Full Gold Standard," *Economic Education Bulletin*, American Institute for Economic Research, March 1961.

Hazlitt, Henry. *The Inflation Crisis and How to Resolve It* (Lanham, MD: University Press of America, 1983).

Kemp, Jack. "The Renewal of Western Monetary Standards," *The Wall Street Journal*, April 7, 1982.

Laffer, Arthur B. and Charles W. Kadlec. "The Point of Linking the Dollar to Gold," *The Wall Street Journal*, October 13, 1981.

Laffer, Arthur B. "Reinstatement of the Dollar: The Blueprint," in Charles W. Kadlec and Arthur B. Laffer (ed.), *The Financial Analyst's Guide to Monetary Policy* (Westport, CT: Praeger Publishing, 1986).

Lee, Susan. "Is Gold the Only Answer?," *Forbes*, September 23, 1985.

Lehrman, Lewis E. "The Case for the Gold Standard," *The Wall Street Journal*, July 30, 1981.

Lehrman, Lewis E. and John Mueller. "Redeem Us with a Cross of Gold," *The Wall Street Journal*, July 8, 1994.

Lehrman, Lewis E. and Ron Paul. The *Case for Gold: Minority Report of the U.S. Gold Commission* (Washington, DC: The Cato Institute, 1982).

McKinnon, Ronald I. "An International Gold Standard Without Gold," *The Cato Journal*, Fall 1988.

Miles, Marc A. *Beyond Monetarism: The Road to Stable Money* (New York: Basic Books, 1984).

Miles, Marc A. "Stabilizing the Dollar in a Global Economy," *The Cato Journal*, Winter 1986.

Mundell, Robert A. "Gold: The Final Asset Problem and Its Resolution," *The International Economy*, H. C. Wainwright & Co. Economics, Inc., February 27, 1980.

Mundell, Robert A. "Gold Would Serve Into the 21st Century," *The Wall Street Journal*, September 30, 1981.

Ranson, R. David. "The Floating Dollar Still Needs an Anchor," *The New York Times*, November 11, 1989.

Reisman, George. "Gold: The Solution to Our Monetary Dilemma," *The Intellectual Activist*, 1980.

"A Return to the Gold Standard," *Business Week*, September 21, 1981.

Reynolds, Alan. "Gold and Economic Boom: Five Case Studies, 1792-1926," in Barry N. Siegel (ed.), *Money in Crisis* (Cambridge: Ballinger Publishing, 1984), pp. 249-68.

Reynolds, Alan. "The Monetary Debate: Stabilize Prices, Not Money," *The Wall Street Journal*, June 29, 1982.

Reynolds, Alan. "Why Gold?," *The Cato Journal*, Spring 1983.

The Role of Gold in the Domestic and International Monetary Systems, U.S. Gold Commission, 1982.

Salsman, Richard M. "Breaking the Banks: Central Banking Problems and Free Banking Solutions," *Economic Education Bulletin*, Vol. XXX, No. 6, American Institute for Economic Research, June 1990.

Salsman, Richard M. "Can Fiat Money Be Managed Effectively?," *Research Reports*, American Institute for Economic Research, June 7, 1993.

Timberlake, Richard H., Jr. "Is the Federal Reserve System Really Necessary?," (Greenwich, CT: Committee for Monetary Research and Education, 1983).

Wanniski, Jude. "A Supply-side Case for a Gold Standard," *Business Week*, December 7, 1981.

White, Lawrence H. "Prospects for Politically Unregulated Money in the United States," *The Political Economy in Perspective*, H. C. Wainwright & Co. Economics, Inc., October 25, 1982.

White, Lawrence H. "Free Banking and the Gold Standard," *Competition and Currency: Essays on Free Banking and Money* (New York: New York University Press, 1989).

Yeager, Leland (ed.). *In Search of a Monetary Constitution* (Cambridge: Harvard University Press, 1962).

To buy publications or find out more about
American Institute for Economic Research please contact us at:

American Institute for Economic Research

250 Division Street

Post Office Box 1000

Great Barrington, MA 01230

Phone: (413) 528-1216

Fax: (413) 528-0103

E-mail: aierpubs@aier.org

On-line: www.aier.org